SOCIAL STRUETURE AND CHANGE AMONG THE HO OF ORISSA

SOCIAL STRUETURE AND CHANGE AMONG THE HO OF ORISSA

By
Dr. K. K. MISRA

GYAN

ISBN : 978-81-212-0080-6

Published, 2018

Published by

Gyan Publishing House
5, Ansari Road
Daryaganj, New Delhi-110002
Phone: 011-47034999, 9811692060
www.gyanbooks.com
E-mail: books@gyanbooks.com

Printed at: G. Print Process, Delhi.

Contents

Preface

Immediately after the Indian independence, all possible efforts are being made by the Government and many other voluntary agencies to ameliorate the plights and tribulations of the indigenous and pre-literate communities of the country and to bring them to the mainstream of Indian nationalism. These tribal populations in our country, which constitute about 7 per cent of the total population and are divided into over 450 communities, have been contributing to the social, economic and cultural life of India since time immemorial. Therefore, their development is of prime concern today, without which our independence would be reduced to a mere slogan. Historically, these communities were under severe deprivation and suppression. During three centuries of British rule, they were not only segregated, but no step whatsoever was taken for their economic or educational development. It is a matter of great satisfaction that our Government is serious enough to see them developed like other Indians, and hence, the plans and policies for tribal development. May be indirectly, for the success of this noble venture, the tentacles of many modern forces are made to engulf the colourful customs and conventions of these communities. Systematic preparation of monographs have been attempted to codify these fast dying traditions and preserve them for the future scholars. The present monograph is an addition to this kind of venture and presents the life and changing customs of the Ho of Mayurbhanj district in Orissa. This tribe mostly inhabits the mining and industrial belt of Bihar-Orissa border and is exposed to the forces of industrialization right from the beginning of the century. From whatever little persistence of their convention exists now and the magnitude of culture change that surreptitiously percolates, one may rightly be apprehensive of the community loosing its identity gradually, and in near future being completely assimilated like many other tribes in India and elsewhere.

The ultimate success of this venture produces many debts —intellectual and otherwise. The field-work was only made possible due to the research grants provided by the University Grants Commission, New Delhi, under its minor research scheme to the University teachers. I am deeply grateful to Professor Dr. L.K. Mahapatra, Professor Dr. N.K. Behura and Professor B.K. Behera of the Department of Anthropology, Utkal University for their constructive criticisms and guidance at various stages of the preparation of the monograph. Entire responsibilities are however mine for any committed error. My colleague, Dr. P.N. Nayak was specially helpful at the post-preparation stage and deserves my gratitude. I am also grateful to Susma and Riki for their unconditional compromise with my long schedules of work at the cost of their comfort. The villagers of Jashipur Block in the district of Mayurbhanj and the officials of Bamanghaty sub-division have helped me to such an extent that without their active cooperation, this work could not have become possible. Finally, I am thankful to Shri J.L. Gupta for taking serious interest in publishing this book so soon and so neatly.

Rakhi Purnima,
Bhubaneswar.

KAMAL K. MISRA

CHAPTER ONE

Introduction and Objectives

A closer look at the development and differentiation of modern sociology and anthropology reveals that these two disciplines fell clearly in the realm of 'environmental' rather than hereditary influence during the second half of the 19th century, when the entire English-speaking world was intellectually pre-occupied with the magical spell of Darwinian biology. Both these disciplines precisely emphasized on the study and analysis of the socio-cultural phenomena, having "...the properties of creating and maintaining a patterned cultural tradition, shared in various ways between the members of living societies and transmitted from generation to generation through learing process and not through biological inheritance" (Parsons, 1965 : 33), which apparently focus on the 'cultural' aspect of the complex. Nevertheless, the disciplines also involved "...organized systems of structured or 'institutionalized' interaction between large number of individuals" (ibid), occupying social positions and discharging social duties and obligations, which might be better called as the 'interactive aspect' of the complex.

This 'cultural' versus 'interactive' aspect of the socio-cultural phenomena and their relative significance in the United States and the U.K., and also in the domains of anthropology and sociology within the U.S.A., has respectively initiated cultural and structural emphases in the sociological studies and analyses. Notwithstanding the empirical interdependence of both these approaches for the conceptualization of social reality, they are made analytically distinct and attempted for, depending on the intellectual inclination of the researchers. The present project, which aims at the study of social structure of a little known tribe in Orissa, i.e., the Ho and the process of change in the social structure due to compelling exogenous and spontaneously operative endogenous factors, should be, therefore, an 'interactive study' in an ideal sense. It should be an interactive study between individuals from among the Ho, occupying certain social positions and playing certain roles which are institutionalized, and the changes therein due to changing physical and socio-cultural environments, to which all the tribes of Orissa are exposed these days. But as has been mentioned earlier, precisely for the difficulty in the compartmentalization of the 'social' and 'cultural' emphases of the present study, some notes of clarification about the concept of 'social structure' seem inevitable.

The concept of social structure has largely been used in the writings of Herbert Spencer, Emile Durkheim, Karl Mannheim and invariably in modern sociological and anthropological literature. In its long course of use since the period of Renaissance till to-date, the concept has undoubtedly undergone a series of refinements and specific, well developed meaning has been attached to the concept by various trend-setters in sociology and anthropology. In spite of all its specifications in scope and usage, the concept is frequently used in its wider connotation, referring indiscriminately to any or all features that contribute to the make up of societies. And Nadel (1957) has rightly observed that the concept of social structure has been used interchangeably with, and becomes a synonym for system, organization, pattern, type and in fact, does not fall very short of 'society as a whole' (Shukla, 1976: 6).

A critique of the development of the concept of social structure reveals that Spencer and Durkheim were responsible for the broad and blanket use of the concept, and were the pioneers in setting the sociological and anthropological traditions in the study of social structure. Nadel (ibid) observes that while in sociology the concept had to rest heavily on the writings of Spencer, in anthropology, Durkheim influenced Radcliffe-Brown, under whose powerful leadership, the discipline of anthropology started picking up a new direction. The widely varied and differing definitions of the concept of social structure stretched out to encompass the whole gamut of socio-cultural phenomena can be established from the following views of some selected but eminent sociologists and anthropologists.

Among the sociologists, Karl Mannheim provides us with a rather philosophical and abstract definition of social structure, when he views the concept as the web of interacting social forces, from which has arisen various modes of observation and thinking. Morris Ginsberg, on the other hand, is highly vocal and explicit in formulating an operational definition of the concept. He defines, "Social structure is concerned with the principal forms of social organization, i.e., types of groups, associations and institutions and the complex of those which constitutes societies" (Ginsberg, 1947 : 8). This apparently seems to be a framework manifesting the integrative pattern of any society under study. A more rational and empirical view of social structure is given by the veteran sociologists, Mac Iver and Page with an explicit emphasis on the social realities, as observed by the researcher right on the field. They define social structure, which "...represent the kind of reality into which we are born and within which we find work and recreation, rewards and penalties, struggle and mutual aid" (Mac Iver and Page, 1962 : 209). T.B. Bottomore endorses the views of Ginsberg in defining social structure as the complex combination of major institutions and groups that constitute the society (Bottomore, 1962 : 111). The aspect of actual human relationships has also found place in explaining the meaning of social structure as : "...all men live with other men in societies and that these societies are entities composed of human relationship structures. This is to say that each society has a pattern of organization composed of the structures resulting from the association of men with each other" (Anderson and Parker,

1964). Among others, Talcott Parsons define social structure as: "In the first instance, it is the kinds of groupings of persons in roles that, combined with their interlacings and criss-crossings, constitute the structure of societies" (Parsons, 1965 : 239). R.K. Merton also defines social structure as comprising the patterned arrangements of role-sets, status-sets and status-sequences (Merton, 1968 : 41-2), which can be compared with the Parsonian interpretation of role relationships.

Although no less difference of opinion exists as regards the definition of social structure in the domain of anthropology, the concept has been used specifically in its comparatively developed and refined meaning than in sociology. Picking up the cue from the writings of his intellectual mentor and particularly, being inspired by the idea of organismic analogy of Durkheim, the British anthropologist, Radcliffe-Brown initially defined social structure in 1937 as the interrelationships or arrangement of 'parts' in some total entity as the 'whole'. In 1950, he explained that the components of social structure are human beings; the structure itself being an arrangement of persons in relationships institutionally defined and regulated. In 1952, he redefined it stating that social structure consisted of human beings not as biological organisms, but as occupying positions in social structure (Refer to Kuper, 1977 : 26-27). Fred Eggan, strongly influenced by Radcliffe-Brown, finds the components of social structure in the inter-personal relations, which become part of the social structure in the form of status and social positions occupied by the individuals in the society. Instead of inter-personal relations, Evans-pritchard searches for the uniformities, regularities and set-order in the social life is the structure of the society (Evans-pritchard, 1979 : 19).

Another important dimension of the concept of social structure comes from the French school of anthropologists, pioneered by Claude Lévi-Strauss. Lévi-Strauss contradicts the view-points of Radcliffe-Brown with the remark that social structure cannot be reduced to an ensemble of social relations, as observed by an anthropologist; rather it is an abstract model built by the researcher, on the basis of observed empirical realities (Bohannan and Glazer, 1973 : 375). Edmund

Leach carries the concept a little further, leaning heavily on the ideal socio-political rules of the society. For him, social structure consists of a set of ideal rules about the distribution of power between persons or groups of persons. This power however refers to the institutionalized and socially regulated power, manifesting the structure of the society. Finally, S.F. Nadel has defined social structure in his own way, with his usual bent on logic and mathematics, that "......it is a property of empirical data—of objects, events or series of events, something they exhibit or prove to possess on observation or analysis; and the data are said to exhibit structure in as much as they exhibit a definable articulation, an ordered arrangement of parts" (Nadel, op. cit.).

The only reason for bringing together all these definitions of social structure from the disciplines of sociology and anthropology is precisely to expose their apparent lack of compatibility and uniformity in conceptualization and explanation. It is, therefore, not an exaggeration to express that any attempt to seek for a mutually agreed and unified definition of social structure will culminate in sheer despair. A synthetic and integrative approach seems to be only viable, which has rightly been told by Robert Redfield (1955) that "Social structure is the holistic concept : the central organizing idea in terms of which everything else in the life of a community so far as proves possible is seen". In this context, however, the explanation given by Evans-pritchard seems equally appropriate that "A total social structure, that is to say the entire structure of a given society, is composed of a number of subsidiary structures or systems, and we may speak of its kinship system, its economic system, its religious system and its political system" (Evans-pritchard, op. cit. : 20).

Both for avoiding a non-consensual definition and meaning of social structure and to expose the socio-cultural phenomena operating in a little-known tribe like the Ho, it was thought that it would be better to use the concept on a very broad social canvas, encompassing the fields of kin network, economy, power and authority, magico-religious beliefs, and the institutions along with ideal role relations for a more comprehensive survey report on the tribe concerned. It is, therefore, more of a monograph than a problem-oriented study, as may be construed at the first glance of the caption.

Like the concept of social structure, social change also entails polemic discussions with a variety of approaches for its study. The evolutionary, structural, dialectical-historical, and institutional approaches (see Singh, 1980) are profusely used for analyzing social change. Ideally, the study of social structure should be followed by structural change, as every society, particularly in the developing countries, rapidly paves the way for a relatively new structure, and more so, in case of the tribal societies. In this report, structural changes in the Ho society are highlighted which however are in line with the commonly held approach of structural change, "......which seeks to explain and not merely describe social change" (ibid).

Justification

As has been mentioned above, the communities of the developing world face the common problem of rapid structural transformation and apparent loss of their traditional values, even to the extent of their identity. Total extinction of some communities both in number and culture has also been noticed. The tribal communities of India in general and Orissa in particular, are equally susceptible to this trend and thus, the need of a monographic survey. Although no monograph was ever published on the Ho of Mayurbhanj in Orissa, sporadic references in the form of short articles on reports reveal that the society has undergone a series of changes in respect of their kin relationships, economic pursuits, polity and religious beliefs. This may be precisely attributed to the fact that Mayurbhanj district in Orissa was open to mine-owners even before Indian independence due to its rich mineral deposits and forest resources. Although mining is no more the bread-earner of the tribals here, its impact not only on their material life, but also on their oral traditions has still remained imprinted. Today a new economic order of salaried job preference and growing elitisation pervades the whole scene in Mayurbhanj, and hence, it was thought to be necessary to record the social and cultural life of the tribe concerned, before it has to lose its peculiar conventional characters.

Further, the district of Mayurbhanj accommodates one-sixth of the total tribal population of the State and has many multi-ethnic villages. The tribe under study, the Ho, has mostly been inhabiting with other tribal communities, although Ho villages are not uncommon. But especially in multi-ethnic villages, the study of preservation and extension of socio-cultural features is of immense help to show the identity and integration of a particular community. Although no attempt has been made in this report to compare the Ho with any other neighbouring tribe, the report is believed to help in such a fruitful comparison.

Methods and Techniques followed

The data were collected through fieldwork by the researcher himself during 1979 and 1980 in the district of Mayurbhanj. Usually, observation—participant and non-participant, interview—structured and unstructured, filling in the schedules and preliminary census forms, collection of case histories and genealogies were followed for data accumulation. Besides the first-hand collection of data, census figures and reports, district gazetteers, administrative reports and other written materials were consulted.

Villages surveyed

The following villages were studied during the said period, where the majority of the population was constituted by the tribe, Ho.

Sub-division	*Tehsil*	*Revenue villages*
Bamanghaty	Rairangpur	Dhangdimuta, Timtima, Digiabeda, Dalki, Dudijharan, Talakpukhri, Bandan, Katubaria
Panchapirh	Karanjia	Jiani, Rugudi, Jamada, Baria, Rangmatia, Nebeda, Khandabandha

CHAPTER TWO

Mayurbhanj : An Ethnic Mosaic

Orissa occupies a significant position in the tribal map of India, accommodating as many as 62 Scheduled Tribes, distributed in all the thirteen districts of the State. According to 1981 census enumeration, Orissa has 59,15,067 Scheduled Tribe population, constituting 22.43 per cent of the total State population, while the proportion of tribal population in the whole of India is around 7 per cent. This shows the magnitude of tribal concentration in Orissa. As per 1971 census, 23.11 per cent of the total State population was constituted by the tribals, and apparently, 1981 census witnesses an increase in the numerical strength of the tribal population in Orissa.

The district of Mayurbhanj has a special distinction of accommodating about one-sixth of the total tribal population of the State. Tribals only constitute 58.56 per cent of the district and thus, it stands first among all the thirteen districts of the State with highest proportion of tribal concentration. The district is the abode of many important tribes of the State, like, the Santal, Ho, Munda, Gond, Bathudi, Birhor, Kharia and many others.

Area, Boundary and Resources

Although Mayurbhanj occupies an area of about 4,022 sq. miles, man has told to have lived on this land for over

50,000 years, which is evident from its large number of early palaeolithic sites and huge remnants of palaeolithic tools. The district is sufficiently rich in the abundance of mineral deposits and forest resources. The iron-ore mines of Gorumahisani, Badampahar and Suleipat have been supporting the steel production in the country since pre-independence times. The district has immense forest resources, which growingly add to the revenue of the State. Similipal range of hills and forests are declared as Tiger Reserves, which not only support wild animals, but also valuable timbers and other forest resources. Mayurbhanj had the distinction of being administered by a ruling family continuously for over thousand years, until the kingdom was merged with the State of Orissa in 1949. The name of the district is derived from two medieval ruling families namely, 'Mayura' and 'Bhanja', who were ruling over the principalities of Bonai and Khijjinga (modern Khiching) respectively.

The district lies between 21°17′ and 22°34′ north latitude and between 85°10′ and 87°10′ east longitude. It is bounded on the north by the Singbhum district of Bihar and Midnapore district of West Bengal, on the south by the districts of Keonjhar and Balasore, on the east by the districts of Balasore and Midnapore, and on the west by the districts of Singbhum and Keonjhar. The district covers an area of 4,021.8 sq. miles with a population of 1,581,873 as per the census enumeration of 1981. There are 912,320 S.T. and 104,057 S.C. population in the district, which constitute 58 per cent and 6.5 per cent approximately of the total population of the district.

The district is divided into four revenue sub-divisions, namely, Baripada, Bamanghaty, Panchpirha and Kaptipada and into five tehsils, namely, Baripada, Betanati, Rairangpur, Karanjia and Udala. The present survey covers the sub-divisions of Bamanghaty and Panchpirha with an intensive focus on the Badampahar P.S., due to its numerical predominance of the Ho population. The S.T. population are scattered all over the district with the following Tehsil-wise distribution :

Baripada	251,410
Betanati	102,305
Rairangpur	226,307
Karanjia	174,769
Udala	157,529

This population is enumerated as 28,429 and 50,764 in the police stations of Badampahar and Jashipur respectively of the district.

The Ho in Mayurbhanj

Although the conflicting naming of the tribes in the census list poses serious difficulty in proper identification of a community, the present survey contemplates on the Ho of Mayurbhanj, which are also named as Larka Kols in Orissa and Bihar. The Larka Kols in the Singbhum district of Bihar are said to have played significant roles against the British action during many millenarian movements in the area. The census of 1971, however, has identified the Ho with 31,916 population, while the Kol, Kolah-Kol-Lohars and Kolha have the numerical strength of 1033, 12194 and 309588 respectively.

This confusion in proper naming of the tribe is due to the use of multiple names to denote the same community. During the period of my fieldwork among the Ho, I had to face the same problem, when they were identified both as the Ho and Kolha in the district of Mayurbhanj. One of my informants explained that the word 'Kolha' is often used by other communities to address them, while the word 'Ho' is used by the Hos themselves to identify their own community. The informant further explained that the indigenous word, Ho, refers to man in general and in that sense, any human being can be designated as a Ho. This view is confirmed by the Report of the Linguistic Survey that *har, hāra, ho* and *koro* are the words commonly used by the Munda tribes to denote themselves (see Russel and Hiralal, III, 1975 : 501).

Migration

The Kolhan region in the Singbhum district of Bihar is recognized and accepted as the place of habitation of this indigenous tribe for a very long period. All the tribal communities of the Chotanagpur plateau are thought to have pushed from the Ganges plain, during the Aryan invasion of north India. These communities probably belonged to the same ancestral stock and there was gradual differentiation and fragmentation during the course of history. Some scholars have observed that the present-day Munda and Kol belong to one original community, except the fact that the Munda are Hinduized and the Kol are commonly those, who "From their jealous isolation for so many years, their independence, their long occupation of one territory, and their contempt for all other classes that come in contact with them, especially the Hindus, probably furnish the best illustration, not of the Mundaris in their present state, but of what, if left to themselves and permanently located, they were likely to become. Even at the present day the exclusiveness of the old Hos is remarkable. They will not allow aliens to hold land near their villages; and indeed if it were left to them no strangers would be permitted to settle in the Kolhan" (Dalton; Quoted in ibid : 502).

Although we do not have any recorded evidence about the migration of the Ho from the Kolhan region to the neighbouring districts of Mayurbhanj and Keonjhar, their migration to Orissa is assumed, basing on the admittance of the members of the community that their ancestors had migrated to Orissa from Kolhan. Even now, their marriage circle in some cases is extended well into Bihar, which reinforces the argument of their possible migration, But, very strangely, notwithstanding their conventional liking towards exclusiveness, they are found in Orissa mostly with other tribal communities in one village. This is never to say that their kin-circle has gone beyond their communal boundary.

The strength of the Ho in Mayurbhanj and their steady increase from 1891 onwards throws light on their possible migration from the Kolhan region. It would be found from the following table that natural increase in every ten years can, perhaps, not account for such an addition in number.

The strength of Ho in Mayurbhanj

Year	*Kol (Ho) population*	*Variation*	*% of variation*	*% of variation to total population of Mayurbhanj*
1891	57,685	—	—	—
1901	67,768	+10,083	17.4	14.7
1911	86,771	+19,003	28.2	19.5
1921	89,183	+ 2,412	2.3	3.4
1931	109,351	+20,168	22.4	17.9
1961	147,230	+37,879	33.9	35.8

Source : The District Gazetteer, 1967.

Language

The Ho language belongs to the austro-asiatic branch of the Austric speech family. As we know, this speech family has two major branches, namely, the austro-asiatic and austronesian. While the Kol or Munda speakers of Bihar and Orissa, Khasi of Assam, Nicobarese and a large number of dialects current in Burma, Siam and Indo-China belong to the former, the latter includes Malayasian and Indonesian languages. The similarity in languages between the tribal populations of India and Southeast Asia has generated many assumptions and speculations about the origin and migration of these groups. Grierson has concluded, "The Mundas, the Mon-Khmer, the wild tribes of the Malay peninsula and the Nicobarese all use forms of speech which can be traced back to a common source though they mutually differ widely from each other". It is, therefore, presumed that had these communities not been the autocthones of India, they must have been migrated from the region of Southeast Asia.

The other languages and dialects resembling the Ho dialect and belonging to the austro-asiatic branch are the Santali, Mundari, Kharia, Bhumij, Korku, Savara and Gadaba. Many neighbouring tribes of the Ho, like that of the Gond, Kondh, Oraon etc. speak Dravidian languages, notwitastanding their locational proximity and similarity in physical features.

Physical Characters

The Ho in general seem to be physically superior to many other tribal communities in Mayurbhanj. Usually, they are dark-brown in complexion with brown eyes. They have long, black, straight or wavy hair. Among the men, the beard is scanty. The average height of an adult male is around 5′6″ while that of the female is about 5′2″. Dr. Haddon has added in case of the Ho of Singbhum that "They are dolicocephalic (C.I. 74.5—76.0) with a long narrow forehead, irregular features, thick lips, eyes often bright and full and not oblique and the nose broad and flat—thus all are platyrrhine" (Quoted in Chatterjee and Das, 1927 : 62). The muscular physique and broad chest development among the men was attributed to : "The constant early use of the bow expanded the chest and set the muscles and their innate passion for the chase over the steep and rugged hills brought their lower limbs into a state of training which the best *phulwan* (wrestler) of the plains of India might envy" (Lt. Tickell, quoted in Singh, 1978 : 9). Although these generalized physical characters are often associated with the Ho, in reality one can find a variety of features due to constant racial admixture, especially with the Aryan blood. In spite of the fact that the Larka Kol had exhibited utmost military skill and aggressiveness during the British days, and their well-built feature may immediately give the impression of toughness, they are found to be extremely hospitable and sober, once the stranger gains the confidence of the community.

Mythical Origin of the Ho

Although some historical accounts of the origin of the tribe have been collected and corroborated by Sir S.C. Roy and Sir William Crooke, the common Ho can only recall the story of mythical origin of his community, and the communities of his near vicinity. There is, in fact, a great deal of similarity in the story of origin, provided by Colonel Tickell, Russel and Hiralal, and that collected from among the local Ho in the district of Mayurbhanj, which are as follows :

After the creation of the plant and animal worlds, *Sing Bonga* (Sun-God), the supreme god of the Ho, thought of creating the most superb and intelligent living being, i.e. the man.

With this view in mind, he created a boy and a girl and put them together in a cave, with the hope that they would eventually procreate to man the world. But with their growing up, there was no sign of passion in them, as they were having brother-sister relations. This pained *Sing Bonga* immensely. One day he put a piece of root collected from the dense jungle in their rice-bowl, when both the brother-sister were not present in the cave. The root, which was put deliberately, had the toxic effect and the rice was automatically converted to rice-beer (*ili*). When the brother and the sister returned back to the cave and consumed the rice-beer, passion was generated and the couple gave birth to twelve pairs of sons and daughters. These pairs ultimately were the progenitors of various communities in the world today. After pairing them, *Sing Bonga* offered them a great variety of food items and the choice in food determined the community. It is told that the pair who chose beef as their food, were the progenitors of the Kol or Ho. Therefore, even today, ceremonial eating of beef and invariably drinking of rice-beer (out of fancy, they call it as their morning tea) are intimately associated with the Ho life and culture.

There is yet another popular version of their origin, which is more or less similar to the one narrated above. The Ho believe, according to this version, that *Sing Bonga* created a male and a female child under a ring stone with an intention to create the human kind through them. Both of them were tied in a brother-sister relationship, and were staying together in the deep forest. *Sing Bonga* was visiting them every now and then, and was their guide in all possible aspects. Days passed by. But it pained the God to note that both of them did not develop required passion to perpetuate the human race. One day *Sing Bonga* told the young boy and the girl that he was gradually getting old, and before he died, he wanted to make them familiar with various forest trees and shrubs for their future use. Accordingly, he gave them roots of some trees and instructed them to put the roots into the half-boiled rice, to wait for 3-4 days, and then to consume it, which would be a healthy drink. The young girl did everything as per the advice. After four days, the rice was fermented and had become bear or *ili*. When they consumed the holy drink, passion generated in them, and they created the human population on the earth. The Ho claim themselves to be their direct descendants. Some of the Ho claim their descent from the famous 'Jara Savara', who had pioneered the worship of Lord Jagannath. There are other versions of their origin also with slight variation, being told by the Ho themselves.

Settlement Pattern

In most of the cases, the Ho villages follow a linear pattern of settlement with two rows of houses facing each other along a common road or foot-track. Every house has its own spacious fenced premises containing the house proper, cow-shed, harvest ground and the storage space for keeping straw and fire-wood. Before selecting a site for their village, the Ho take into account the nearness of water source and forest. Each Ho village has a *jahera than* or the place for their village deity, which is usually a big sal groove, located preferably in the easternly direction of the village.

House Type

The typical Ho house has either one multi-purpose room or 2-3 rooms at the most. If it is a one-roomed house, it is partitioned to atleast three small spaces by a temporary thin wall. One of these spaces is used as kitchen, while the other two are used for storing grains and for multi-purpose use. If the house has more than one room, every room is separate in its function. The doors are either wooden or bamboo, and windows are conspicuously absent in most of the cases. The entrance of the house is ideally towards the east, although it is not strictly adhered to. The roof is thatched and mud floor is common. The walls are either bamboo-made or from a local variety of shrub, plastered with mud. The walls are painted with yellow or red coloured mud, which are locally available.

The selection of house site is done meticulously and with utmost caution. The Ho perform a ritual for the purpose with the help of the village *dehuri* and elder members of the lineage. The proposed site is inspected to ensure its nearness to the water source. Then a small patch in the site is cleared and is anointed with cow-dung paste. In the evening they leave some ritualized grains of sun-dried rice and visit the place the next morning. If they find the rice undisturbed or not significantly disturbed, the site is thought to be auspicious for the house construction. After the selection of the site, a bamboo pole is erected at the central place of the site with some straw and mango leaves at the top of the pole, in order to publicize its possession. Normally, other people do not encroach upon the site, if a pole is erected.

Dress Pattern

The dress pattern of the Ho is very simple and not remarkably distinct from that of their neighbours like the Santal, Bathudi, Munda etc. The male members use a coarse *dhoti*, hand woven, and rarely coming below the knees. The lower portion of the *dhoti* is tucked at the back. Modern types of dresses like synthetic trousers, shirts etc. are used by the village youth frequently.

The women have also a very simple pattern of dress. They use a piece of coarse *sari*, usually with broad coloured criss-crosses and is about six feet to eight feet long. One end of the *sari* reaches down upto the knee level as a lower garment, while the other end is held tightly covering the breast area across the left shoulder and below the right arm-pit. Use of blouses and under-garments is not uncommon among young girls and also those working outside the village. The women use a good number of ornaments including glass or silver bangles, bead or glass or silver necklaces, silver anklets, hair pins, wristlets etc. Use of ear rings and silver rings in their fingers is also common. The face and arms of the women folk are sometimes covered with tatoo marks of different kinds, which are gradually becoming unpopular these days.

Food Habit

Rice constitutes the staple food of the Ho. Dehusked rice, which is done almost every day in all the houses, is used. Fried leaves of various kinds, onion, garlic, chillies and a pinch of salt constitute the typical side dish. Sometimes they prepare rice cakes also. They relish fishes collected from the nearby water source. Meats of sheep, goat, hares, deer, fowls, pigeons, ducks, geese etc. are boiled and taken with great satisfaction.

Although beef and pork are sometimes taken, increasingly they avoid eating these. The Ho prepare a drink of home made rice beer or *ili*, and is consumed by every body irrespective of their sex and age. The beer prepared from Mohua leaf is also a favourite drink of the Ho. For the preparation of the rice beer a tablet, locally known as *ranu* is prepared from the roots of some jungle shrubs, which helps in the fermentation of the cooked rice. No festival or ritual among the Ho is complete without rice beer and meat of some kind or the other.

Hunting, Fishing and Agricultural Implements

Hunting is a part of the culture of the Ho. The observance of annual communal hunting expedition in the month of *Baisakh* (April-May) among them till these days, signifies the place of hunting in their social life. Bow and arrow of various kinds are used in hunting expeditions. The bow is usually bamboo made and the arrow has sharp iron tip and the shaft is of bamboo or can. Feathers of birds are used in the butt end of the arrow to enhance its speed. Communal and individual fishing is also very common among the Ho. Use of fishing nets, woven either in synthetic or cotton threads, is common. Bamboo fishing nets are also used among the Ho. As the Ho are primarily agriculturists, the use of wooden and iron agricultural implements is very common. Wooden plough with iron blade, wooden yoke, moi (for levelling the field) are commonly used items during agricultural operation. Iron axe, knives, sickles etc. are also used by the Ho. Other household articles and utensils are prepared out of wood, bamboo, cane, brass, aluminium and bell-metal.

Although the pattern of culture of the Ho closely resembles with that of the other neighbouring communities, in many respects they maintain their self-identity. Rapid proliferation of urbanisation and industrialisation has brought about many consequential changes in them, but a Ho feels proud to identify himself as a Ho, remembering the bravery of his predecessors in Kolhan during the British Raj.

Earlier Writings on the Ho

There have been many writings on the tribe Ho, both

during pre and post-independence periods, describing their socio-cultural life and values, despite an apparent terminological confusion between 'Ho', 'Kol', 'Kolha' and 'Larka Kol' etc. Most often, these terms have been used interchangeably to denote a single group of people inhabiting different areas, and sometimes, the terms are found to be used for a group of tribals, as they are designated by the surrounding population.

The bulk of the writings on the Ho, during the pre-independence days, is precisely due to the fact that they had drawn the attention of many, particularly the British administration, owing to their active participation and brave encounter with the British troops during a series of tribal insurrections in the Chotanagpur region. Further, the writings on the Ho before the independence and even after, are contempleted on the group inhabiting the Kolhan region in Singbhum district of Bihar, which has been regarded as the original seat of the Ho or Kolha. Although it has been established that the Ho have migrated in all directions in course of time, and also to the bordering district of Mayurbhanj in Orissa, no significant study has been made on the tribe, to note their adaptation to the changing ecological and socio-cultural environment. But, in any case, the studies conducted in Bihar and Madhya Pradesh on the Ho or Kolha, have been a great asset in understanding their way of life.

The initial attempt was, perhaps, made by the British administrator and writer, Col. E.T. Dalton in 1872, in the pages of his monumental work, *Descriptive Ethnology of Bengal.* Dalton has very aptly observed the basic personality of the Ho or Larka Kol as of those, who "From their jealous isolation for so many years; their independence, their long occupation of one territory, and their contempt for all other classes that come in contact with them, especially the Hindus, probably furnish the best illustration, not of the Mundaris in their present state, but of what, if left to themselves and permanently located, they were likely to become. Even at the present day the exclusiveness of the old Hos is remarkable. They will not allow aliens to hold land near their villages; and indeed if it were left to them no strangers would be permitted to settle in the Kolhan" (Dalton, 1872).

The pioneering attempt by Dalton was followed by Sir H.H. Risley in *The Tribes and Castes of Bengal* (1891) and Russel and Hiralal in *The Tribes and Castes of the Central Provinces of India* (1916). The latter distinguish the Kol or Ho as "A great tribe of Chota Nagpur, which has given its name to the Kolarian family of tribes and languages. A part of the district of Singbhum near Chaibasa is named the Kolhan as being the special home of the Larka Kols, but they are distributed all over Chota Nagpur, whence they have spread to the United Provinces, Central Provinces and Central India" (1975 : 500). They have discussed in greater detail their legend of origin, strength, sub-divisions, totemism, marriage customs, religion, witch-craft, funeral rites, inheritance, physical appearance, dances, social rules and offences, caste panchayat, occupation and language etc. This long account by Russel and Hiralal was perhaps the most exhaustive description on the tribe at the time of its publication in 1916.

Census operations in British India had also contributed immensely not only to the population figures, but also to the knowledge of manners and customs of various tribal groups in India. Under the banner of Census of India, some other Britishers wrote on the Ho like B.C. Allen in 1901, L.S.S. O' Malley in 1911, P.C. Talents in 1921 and A.E. Porter in 1931. M. Laeequddin and A. Mitra also supplemented to this effort in their short reports in the Census of Mayurbhanj State, 1931 and Census of West Bengal, 1951 respectively. Notwithstanding their inadequacy, these reports have been the sources of intellectual insight for the future researchers.

The first book on the Ho was published in 1927 with a title, *The Hos of Seraikella*, by the University of Calcutta and under the authorship of A. Chatterjee and T.C. Das. It was an outcome of an excursion into the Ho country of Seraikella by the members of the Deptt. of Anthropology, Calcutta University in 1925. The work is undoubtedly an excellent anthropological treatise of the Ho way of life and social structure, with an apparent thrust on the nature and extent of change among them, as a result of constant Hindu impact on their traditional culture and value system. The data have been collected by a rigorous field-work and analyzed meticulously, as is usually done in an anthropological work. The book covers the Ho village organization, daily life, manner and customs, ossuaries, kinship and social organization, religion and physical characters.

In the pre-independence India, the Christian missionaries working in various interior, tribal areas of the country had a commendable contribution to the repository of knowledge in Indian anthropology. W.G. Griffiths, a missionary of the methodist Church at Jubbulpore brought out a book in 1946 titled, *The Kol Tribes of Central India*, published by the Royal Asiatic Society of Bengal. Long association of Griffith with the local Kols evoked a spirit of scholarship in him, and eventually, the book came to the limelight. In this book, the author has categorically distinguished the Kols of Central India from that of the Chotanagpur region and he writes, "The Tribe itself should be carefully distinguished from the Munda tribes of Chota Nagpur which are frequently called Kols in their generic sense. There is no specific Kol tribe in that area, although there is a group called the Larka Kols, or Hos, famous for an insurrection in the year 1832, and a part of the district of Singbhum is called the Kolhan after them" (Griffiths, 1946 : 1). He has accepted the proposition that Rewa State has been the place of Kol concentration.

D.N. Majumdar, later in 1950, wrote a book under the title, *The Affairs of a Tribe*, as an outcome of his series of field-works in the Kolhan region of Bihar for almost over 25 years. The book vividly reflects the flawless collection of anthropological materials on the Ho by Majumdar over these years. It is, so far, the outstanding work on the Ho of Bihar and a milestone in the anthropological career of Majumdar. Recently also, in 1978, a book is published titled, *The Ho Tribe of Singbhum* by C.P. Singh, which is more of a historical account than anthropological, despite some valuable contributions to their pattern of culture in general. It is apparent therefore that all the books discussed above reveal the culture of the Ho in Bihar and Madhya Pradesh, and even a single book has not been published on the Ho of Orissa so far.

Besides published books and reports on the Ho, there are many research articles appeared in some very reputed Indian anthropological journals like, *Man in India, Journal of the Asiatic Society of Bengal, Bulletin of the Cultural Research Institute* (West Bengal), *Vanyajati, The Eastern Anthropologist, Adivasi, Bulletin of the Bihar Tribal Research Institute, Journal of the Bihar and Orissa Research Society,* and in some other journals like *Indian Journal of Medical Research.*

Although the oldest research article on the Ho, published in India, with a title, "Ho Folklore" was written by S. Haldar in 1915 and appeared in *Journal of the Bihar and Orissa Research Society*, followed by an article on "Ho Auguries" in 1917 in the same journal, the largest number of research articles on the Ho was written by Majumdar between 1925 and 1950. Majumdar's articles covered the entire gamut of Ho culture including articles on their traditional origin, description of their *bongas*, kinship terminology, physical characters, birth ceremonies, outdoor and sedentary games, marriage and betrothal rites, death and connected ceremonies, worship festivals, religious life and anthropometric comparison between the Ho and Saora. His contribution is no doubt outstanding to the study of Ho culture in Kolhan, which is an entire life-time's dedicated research on the tribe concerned.

Among others, G. Chattopadhyay, S. Biswas and B.C. Roy Chaudhuri, individually or jointly, contributed immensely to our knowledge of Ho festivals, their traditional concept of diseases, kinship and marriage, and their name-giving ceremony, between 1955-1965. While B.K. Das Gupta (1958) focussed on Ho ceremonial hunting, G.S. Roy added more on their religious beliefs and magical practices during 1954-60. The studies on the Ho Folklore were not left out by the researchers. Besides Haldar (1915) on folklore, Deogan (1928) and Mitra (1917) contributed to the Ho folktales, and Mitra (1926) and Sarkar (1916, 1919) to Ho riddles.

Valuable contributions of Dhan (1961), Hutton (1951),

Macpherson (1930), Mitra (1942), Pradhan, (1963-64), Misra (1982-83), Prasad (1961), Sahu (1951) and some others to various aspects of the Ho society and culture have enriched the knowledge on the tribe concerned. But again, most of these articles are on the Ho of Bihar, excepting only a couple of them, which is the State of the Ho concentration. The present work, despite its obvious inadequacies, is an attempt on the Ho of Orissa, where the tribe is found amidst other tribal groups in a new sorrounding.

CHAPTER THREE

Kinship and Social Organization

Every known society in the world, irrespective of their technological development, are organized to ensure effective implementation of the prevailing norms and the maintenance of perfect harmony. But in the case of technological simpler societies, we come across the evidence of high respect for the norms and values, which eventually culminate in highly integrated and well-disciplined structures. The Ho society, a patrilineal and patriarchal one, is divided extensively into various sub-groups for the purpose of closely knit relations between the members and to avoid indiscriminate marriage or sexual union.

Clan Organization

Barring a few exceptions, most of the societies are divided into clans. The clan may be defined as "...an exogamous division of a tribe the members of which are held to be related to one another by some common tie, it may be belief in descent from a common ancestor, common possession of a totem or habitation of a common territory" (*Notes and Queries in Anthropology*). Although in Mayurbhanj, any bipolar division of the Ho society into superior and inferior halves was never noticed, as observed by Chatterjee and Das (1927 : 40) in Seraikella, the society is found to be extensively divided into numerous clans or *kili*, as they name it. One of the informants, Shri Bhagaban Chhattar, has provided with an exhaustive list of 90 *kilis*, that he could remember at the time of interview (see

Appendix I for the list of clans). Prior to this, however, Majumdar (1926: 154) and Chatterjee and Das (op. cit. : 88-94) had given the lists of 53 and 86 *kilis* of the Ho respectively.

Unlike many other tribal villages, having corporate kin-groups, the Ho village is usually of multi-ethnic and multi-clan. This composition, in a way, is necessary to keep the rival clans balanced. A Ho *kili* is strictly exogamous in nature and even a little violence in the form of either pre-nuptial or post-marital sexual relation leads to the extent of excommunication in such a sexually liberal society. The clan exogamy is due to the fact that the members of a *kili* are believed to be descended from a common mythical ancestor and thus, are related to each other by blood tie. This belief in blood relation not merely imposes a total ban on marital relations, but also induces high degree of unity and intimacy between the members of a *kili*. Every *kili* is associated with a totem, which though not totally avoided, is treated with deference. It was not possible to collect the totems of all the 90 clans, as the informants were not aware of them. However, the totems of some clans were collected as :

Purti	Crocodiles
Hasda	Wild goose
Hembram	Tree, bearing berries
Tiu	Jackal

The *kili* of a Ho is easily discernible due to the common use of clan name as his surname. But the confusion lies in the ethnic identification of the individual. Because, the Santal, Munda and other neighbouring communities are also having clans with similar names, and in most cases, with similar totems. While a male member of the Ho retains his clan identity throughout his life, a female member has to change her clan after the marriage. But in case of the remarriage of a widow, the parental clan is adhered to, rather than the clan of her deceased husband.

Lineage

The Ho *kili*, as in some other tribes, is not territorially delimited, and the possible reason being the migration of the members of the community from Singbhum to Mayurbhanj and Keonjhar of Orissa. It is, in fact, not possible to find out the Ho groups, belonging to all the 90 clans collected in Mayurbhanj. However, a clan in a Ho village is represented by one or two lineages, the members of which constitute a corporate kin group and eventually form an unified and integrated kin circle. The eldest male member of the lineage is honoured by the junior members, and he represents the lineage in the matters relating to the interests of its members. These days although no property is left to be shared by the lineage members, and apparently the head of the lineage has no role whatsover to play in this regard, his age and experience only accrue the honour that he gets. Even the introduction of new polity of democracy through adult franchise, has drastically reduced the responsibility of a secular head in case of a lineage elder.

Family

The family is regarded as the smallest socio-economic-politico-religious unit among the Ho, like all other tribal and non-tribal communities. From the present survey in Mayurbhanj, it is estimated that more than 70 per cent of the Ho families are nuclear in composition. Families in the pattern of Hindu joint families are found to some extent, and mostly in cases, where affluency exists. Growing number of nuclear families may be an emerging trend due to increasing economic compulsion and stringent needs, because of the fact that Chatterjee and Das (op. cit. : 48) account for the predominance of joint families among the Ho of Seraikella. As usual, the nuclear family consists of the parents and their unmarried sons and daughters, while the joint family accommodates the married brothers and their children. Monogamy among the Ho is a common practice with rare occurrence of polygynous families. Although polygyny is never encouraged in a Ho community, it takes place in exceptional situations like the barren or disabled first wife. The supremacy of the first wife nevertheless is maintained and the second wife is only sought for with her approval. The father is recognized as the head of the family and all authorities relating to the overall maintenance of the family is vested to him. He officiates in all the family rituals and represents the family in village functions.

Inter-personal relations perpetuate between the members of the family, which is based on cordiality, mutual love, affection and sympathy. Even when the married sisters are divorced by their husbands, they usually get back to the natal family and remain there either till the dispute is settled any way or they are remarried elsewhere.

As an economic unit, the family functions under the leadership of the father. The wife, besides her regular responsibilities of household works and child-care, assists the husband in agricultural operations and sometimes engaging herself as a daily wager to supplement the family income. Unmarried grown up daughters also contribute immensely to the family economy. Till his death, the father maintains his supremacy as the head of the family. After his death, all the movable and immovable properties are distributed among the sons and they get separated according to their respective convenience. The eldest son usually gets a little more landed property than his usual share, due to the fact that all family friends and relatives pay their visit to the residence of the eldest son in case of any family festival.

Descent

Descent among the Ho is strictly traced unilineally and unilaterally, and thus, the Ho is basically a patrilineal society, where descent is through the male line. All the members of the society are agnatic kin to each other. As mentioned earlier, parental property—movable and immovable, family surname and special family distinctions, if any, are transmitted from the father to the son. This principle constitutes the patri-lineage and patri-clan among the Ho.

Kin Groups

Although the Ho recognize relatives upto the seventh degree, the intensity of relations and interaction continues upto the third degree very well. Of course, decreasing intensity of relations is apparent, when one moves from the primary to the tertiary kin groups.

The primary relatives or the relatives of the first order, usually sharing a household, foster highest degree of intensity in inter-personal relations and integrity, so far as daily activities are concerned. While the local secondary relatives, like the cousins of the paternal side, constitute one single corporate kin group with sharing of mutual love and affection; the distant secondary relatives like MB, FZ, in-laws and other affines maintain the relation with frequent visit and offering occasional presentations during social ceremonies. They are never avoided during the celebration of life-cycle rituals and other festivities. The tertiary relatives, who are the secondary relatives of a primary kin, such as, FZH, MBW etc. usually meet during marriage or mortuary rituals and communal festivals. Here also, there is the custom of gift giving and exchange of goodwill, which keeps on maintaining the spirit of integrity.

Kinship Terminology

Kin terms among the Ho were collected from Badampahar and Sukuruli Gram Panchayats in the district of Mayurbhanj and were cross-checked to find out the similarities and discrepancies. The difference was found to be meagre, excepting the modern use of certain kin terms due to the impact of neighbouring caste communities. Example may be cited in case of *dada*, which now refers to the elder brother, while the conventional use of *unding kua* is still in vogue in many areas. A list of kin terms is, however, attached at the end of this report under Appendix II.

The analysis of kin terms used by the Ho reveals that excepting 4 terms coming under the descriptive system, rest others belong to the classificatory system. The descriptive terms are : *Buba* (father), *Maa* (mother), *Ham/Hamin/Gosian* (husband) and *Era* (wife). Even a cursory look at the classificatory kin terms indicates some prevailing social norms in the Ho society and also the expected or ideal pattern of behaviour. The use of the terms like *Hatom* to address FZ, MBW and WM ; and *Muman* or *Kamu* to address MB, FZH and WF hints about the prevailing practice of preferential cross-cousin marriage among them. Here, apparently, the criterion of affinity is ignored, which culminates in these classificatory terms. Further, the use of same word, *Kaka* for FB (yr.) and MZH, and *Kaki* or *Gaen* for FBW and MZ indicates the possibility of group marriage.

In second descending generation, sometimes the criterion of sex is ignored and hence, a common word, *Jaain*, is used for all the SS, DS, DD and SD. There is no blurring of relative age, the considaration of which gives rise to different kin terms for elder and younger husband's sister and sister's husband.

Lineal and collateral kinsmen are differentiated among the Ho, both in terminology and behaviour. Application of three different terms for Father (*buba*), Father's brother (*kaka*) and Mother's brother (*kuman*) indicates a bifurcate collateral type of terminological system.

Although there have been changes in the kin terms due to the impact of many neighbouring communities, the traditional terms are not totally forgotten and even, most of the terms are common with that used in Kolhan of Bihar.

Kinship Usages

Certain restrictions in kin behaviour between the members of a community help in maintaining healthy relationships and to avoid unwanted bitterness. On the other hand, mutual joking behaviours in some cases are prescriptive to normalize any kind of strain that may come on the way of harmonious relations between the members. These behaviours are institutionalized and accepted by the community as a whole.

Joking relations, among the Ho, exist between the elder brother's wife (*hili*) and the husband's younger brothers and sisters(*eril*). This kind of relations are also found between elder sister's husband(*tenyang*) and wife's younger sister (*tenyang kui*) and wife's younger brother (*tenyang*) ; grand-parents and grand-children. Since the role-playing members in the first two examples belong to the same generation, they feel free to joke each other, which helps mitigating any kind of misunderstanding between them. These pairs also constitute potential marital partners, culminating in levirate and sorrorate marriages.

Avoidance with some relatives is also customary among the Ho, although the intensity and uniformity of avoidance is not that rigid, as observed in a Hindu caste. However, the relations between younger brother's wife (*kimining*) and the husband's elder brother (*bau hanyar*) ; wife's elder sister and younger sister's husband etc. are the relations of avoidance. Usually they do not appear before each other and touch each other. A Ho woman normally avoids the elderly male members of the lineage as a mark of respect and reverence. There are, however, violations in the prescriptive avoidances, most often during the quarrel between a *kimining* and a *bau hanyar*.

Teknonymy is also not uncommon among the Ho. When husband's elder sister (*aji hanaring*) addresses her brother's wife (*hili*), it is commonly not by the recognized terminology, but as the mother of such and such (the name of the eldest son/daughter being normally used). Similarly, mutual addressing of husband and wife is mediated by the names of their sons or daughters.

CHAPTER FOUR

Means of Subsistence and Economy

The early history of the tribe reveals that the Ho were subsisting on hunting of wild animals and gathering of roots, fruits and tubers from the forest, while their abode was the dense jungles of the Chotanagpur plateau. Gradually, due to increasing contact with the Hindu caste communities, they started practising incipient, and finally plains-land wet agriculture. Even in Mayurbhanj, the Ho confess that they were exclusively depending upon hunting and gathering after their migration from the Kolhan region and due to close association with a caste community, the Mahato, they learned the techniques of agriculture. But the abundance of land around their place of habitation, made them complacent to acquire and later, the policy of forest reservation, left them almost landless.

Although, generally speaking, the Ho are considered to be settled agriculturists, the situation around Badampahar and Gorumohisani is a little different. Much before Indian independence, in the year 1910, the TISCO (Tata Iron and Steel Co.) banked upon these mines for extracting iron-ore, which were the mother-mines of the Company. The Ho and other tribal communities within a radius of 15-20 kms were allured by the remunerative daily waging and preferred to be engaged as daily labourers. There is no doubt that employment in mines and eventual cash earning exposed these tribals to the evils of an urban-industrial culture. Agriculture was mostly an occupation of the old and disabled. Whatever landed property was being possessed, ultimately went into the clutches of money-lenders and affluent caste Hindus. But when the mines operation under the TISCO came to an end in the year 1968, and large scale extraction was reduced to nothing, it had a long lasting impact on the Ho. Landlessness coupled with high aspirations compelled them to abandon their native villages and settle in distant mining areas like Daitari and Sukinda in Cuttack district. The table on page 32, however, provides us with the present pattern of occupation among the Ho from the statistics collected from the selected villages around Badampahar and Jashipur.

The table shows that out of 532 workers, 274 are engaged as daily labourers in different mines, factories etc., 159 depend on agriculture, 45 still eke out their living from nearby forests, and 39 are service-holders in different offices of the Government and private enterprises. Therefore, daily labourers constitute 51.50%, agriculturists 29.9%, forest collectors 8.4%, service-holders 7.4% and 2.8% is constituted by those, who are engaged in other means like menial services, hawking, domestic services etc.

Ho Method of Agriculture

Although daily labour in mines and factories has allured the Ho to a great extent, some of them have taken up agriculture as their major means of subsistence. Around 30% of the Ho still depend on plains-land agriculture, as per the statistics collected from around Badampahar. Land is their primary resource in this regard.

When the Ho came into contact with the Mahato, a Hindu caste group, probably migrants from the Midnapore district of West Bengal, the Ho could become settled and skilled agriculturists. Initially, they constituted an agricultural labour group under the land-owning Mahatos. The reluctance in acquiring land among the Ho was the perpetual fear to pay heavy land-tax to the Government, the fear psychosis being created by the cunning and intelligent Mahatos to see the Ho as mere labourers. However, land ownership or landlessness made hardly any difference to the common Ho, when the settle-

Pattern of Occupation among the Ho

Village	*Total No. of Households*	*No. of Ho Households*	*Total No. of Ho Workers*	*Agricultural*	*Daily Labour*	*Collection*	*Service*	*Miscellaneous*
Jiani	39	9	30	4	12	4	2	8
Rangamatia	28	7	24	2	8	7	7	—
Baria	296	74	193	65	95	30	3	—
Dhangidimuta Badasahi	198	39	135	43	72	—	13	7
Dhangidimuta Sanasahi	128	24	92	30	51	2	9	—
Timtima	108	22	58	15	36	2	5	—

ments were surrounded by dense forests and the Ho had an unchallenging expertise in bow and arrow operation. But when the surrounding forest gradually declined and the ban was imposed by the Government on the use of forest by the tribals, the Ho felt the necessity of land as a resource. Nevertheless, when the popular Government of India granted the acquiring of 5 acres of land to every landless tribal family out of the unused Government land, some of them could possess a little landed property. The table on page 34 indicates the landed property owned by the Ho, in different villages around Jashipur and Badampahar.

The Ho classify land into three types, mainly depending on the elevation of the land surface. These are :

(1) *Da Ate* : *Da ate* is the Ho term for the low land or wet land, which has some kinds of facilities for getting sufficient water for the crop. Sometimes, the land below the stream bed and usually, the land nearer to a perennial stream come under this category. For water management, the Ho prepare embankments, which ensure sufficient supply of water in the command areas. Late varieties of paddy and seasonal vegetables are grown in this kind of land, which are usually multi-cropped ones.

(2) *Dhipa Ate* : This type of land refers to the rain-fed category, which do not have any facility for irrigation. In fact, most of the land in my area of survey come under this category. When these land are quite high up on the bank of a river, the Ho prepare embankments at different places down the stream and lift water through a local system of water lifting, based on the principle of lever, which is termed as *tenda*. During the summer, these land are used for growing vegetables and other crops like chilly, sugar-cane etc. But normally, one crop of early variety of paddy is grown in these land.

(3) *Goda Ate* : This refers to the hill slopes and used by the Ho in growing mainly pulses and oilseeds. Black gram (*raba*), red gram (*rahi*) and many other local varieties like, *kesari*, *gudula*, *tisi*, *ruma*, *jangjada* etc. are grown from the

Landed Property of the Ho

Land in Acres	*Jiani*	*Rangmatia*	*Baria*	*Dhangidimuta Badasahi*	*Dhangidimuta Sanasahi*	*Timtima*
Upto 0.5	5	1	17	10	7	2
0.5—1.0	1	0	22	10	3	6
1.0—1.5	3	0	18	5	2	6
1.5—2.0	0	4	5	5	8	0
2.0—2.5	0	2	2	4	1	4
2.5—3.0	0	0	6	2	2	2
3.0—3.5	0	0	2	1	1	1
3.5—4.0	0	0	2	1	0	1
4.0—4.5	0	0	0	1	0	0

uplands. As these varieties do not require so much of water, upland is most suitable for these varieties.

From their kitchen gardens, invariably attached to every Ho homestead, they get brinjal (*benga*), tomato (*biliti*), greens (*aya*), beans (*simili*), papaya (*bindi daru*) and many other fruits and vegetables.

Labour in Agriculture

The *modus operandi* of the Ho agricultural production is not very different from the other tribal communities of the district. Although individuality has taken over the spirit of traditional collectivity in the Ho social life, communal labour still plays an important role in agricultural production. In some villages, some members of a lineage, including women and children of both sexes, constitute a labour group, especially during transplantation, harvest and transfer of crops from the field to the granary. Ideally, the members of this labour group do not get anything in cash or kind excepting the mid-day meal, offered by the land-owner. The group works on a rotation basis and therefore, each member is a beneficiary of this labour group. Requisition of the bullocks of some lineage members at different phases of agricultural operation is done, when no rent is paid for the services rendered by these animals. But this guarantees reciprocal help at the time of need. Quite often, other lineage members of the village are also requested to participate in this joint venture, even though the response may not be in affirmative due to obvious reasons. These days, in most of the cases, there is hired labour for the agricultural operations. While an adult male gets Rs. 5 as daily wage, a female gets Rs. 3. The payment may be in cash or in kind, depending on the demand of the labourer.

Agricultural Cycle

The cycle of agriculture among the Ho is not different from that of other neighbouring tribal and caste communities. It starts with the processing of the field during the months of May-June, just before the arrival of south-west monsoon. Sowing is usually done during June, while transplantation of paddy (*rayate male*) becomes necessary at least once, during August and then, they keep vigilant watch on the field till the harvest in the months of November-December.

Associated Rituals

Two significant rituals, associated with agriculture, are observed among the Ho. The first one is observed before the harvest of the crop and the household head selects an auspicious day in consultation with the *dehuri* or the village priest. On this pre-arranged day, the eldest male member of the family goes to the field after taking bath. He carries with him vermilion, sun-dried rice and three chickens of black, brown and white colours. He sacrifices in the field the black one to *Kalikuduru*, brown one to *Laxmithakurani* and white one to *Pitasuni*, who are responsible for the protection of the field and a better harvest. The second festival is commonly known as *Jamnam* or *Nuakhia*, observed during the month of Ashwina (October-November) for the first rice eating of the session. This is a communal festival, unlike the first one, and a date is fixed by the *dehuri* for the occasion. On the stipulated date, a communal feast is arranged and the village goddess (*Grama Siri*) is propitiated for better harvest in the ensuing years.

Hunting

Hunting now-a-days has become more of a ritual than a means of subsistence among the Ho. Individual hunting is no more in practice due to deforestation and reservation of left over forests.

Communal hunting, a symbol of social integrity and cooperation is still being practised by the Ho. Usually after the *akhami trutiya* or *akshya trutiya* in the month of baisakh (April-May), all the male members of the village move for hunting expedition to the forest under the leadership of the village *dehuri*. They even cover a distance of 25 to 30 kilometres during this expedition. A camp is soon established in the forest for the purpose. The *dehuri* propitiates the forest deity (*buru bonga*) with the sacrifice of a black chicken. As per his direction, the group starts an intensive search of the game. After the hunting, the head of the game goes to the *dehuri* and the actual hunter of the animal gets a little more with his share.

Then, there is equidistribution of meat among all the participants. The group never comes empty-handed in the fear of being teased and humiliated by the womenfolk of the village.

Collection

Natural forest is almost non-existing around the area, where the present survey was being undertaken. In course of time, mostly due to the timber smugglers and partly due to indiscriminate felling of valuable trees by the local communities, the area is only left with barren hillocks and undlauted land surface. Recently, of course, due to the implementation of social forestry programmes, most of the villages are surrounded by juvenile forests, which are maintained and managed by the villagers to meet their minimum needs like fuel and shelter. But, there are Ho settlements inside the similipal range of hills, where the people almost subsist on forest resources. The major forest products include timber, fire-wood, leaves, edible fruits, roots and tubers, honey, gums, resins, lac, silk cocoon, wax, arrowroot and many other valuable items. The flowers of mohua (*matkan*), sal (*sarjam ba*) and many fruits of local variety, such as, *berri bakara*, *kada*, *lawa daru*, *hesa daru*, *jaja daru* (tamarind), *uli daru* (mango) are collected from the forest. The edible roots and tubers include wild potato (*unur sanga*), *pitalu*, *marang sanga*, *tungam sanga*, *bedai sanga*, *chhiligodi sanga*, *kuchhui sanga*, *gosam sanga* etc. *Sabai* grass is abunduntly found in these forests, which is collected for rope-making and selling them in local markets. The flowery stick of a plant, *sairi*, is also collected the cluster of which is used as broom.

The division of labour in collection is quite neat among the Ho. The difficult and risky collection like that of honey, lac etc. and cutting of timbers are taken up by the male members, and collection of flowers, fruits, seeds, leaves, roots and tubers, and fire-wood is mostly left to the women and children.

Fishing

Fishing is also not a significant alternative of subsistence for the Ho, precisely because mostly this needs concerted efforts by a number of individuals, and further, it cannot be relied upon always due to the drying up of springs and other water resources. However, during leisure hours, the Ho move towards the nearby stream or river or pond for fishing. Fish is termed as *haku* in the Ho dialect. Various kinds of fishing nets and bamboo-made traps are designed by the Ho for fishing. Some of the varieties of fish, reported by the Ho include *mohu haku, katla haku, kan haku, suli haku, baya haku, kentia haku, ha haku, thar haku* etc. Besides fishes, big or small, tortoise (*har*), snail (*genda*) and other aquatic varieties are relished by the Ho.

Daily or Contract Labour

From the areas surveyed, it was found that 51.50% of the total Ho workers are engaged as labourers. Usually they work in the iron-ore mines, china-clay mines and small factories around the area. It was found that near Jashipur, on the bank of the river Khairi-Bhandon, a china-clay factory has been established by the private endeavour. The daily labourers of the factory used to get Rs. 5.50 as their wage, irrespective of their sex. But besides mines and factories, the forest contractors normally recruit daily wagers for cutting, transporting, loading and unloading of timbers, bamboos at various places. The wage here also ranges from Rs. 5.50 to Rs. 6.50 for the male workers and Rs. 4.50 to Rs. 5.50 for the female workers. Normally, the payment is weekly and in case of emergency, the contractor pays some amount as an advance. Almost all the adult members of a Ho household in the vicinity of Jashipur and Badampahar work as labourers and supplement the income of the family.

Expenditure

The major expenditure among the Ho is essentially to meet the requirements of the daily ration. If an individual prepares two square meals a day, the expenses even fall short of the daily income as a labourer, keeping aside other expenditures, like, clothing, house maintenance, meeting social obligations etc.

Indebtedness

Out of the total 175 households surveyed in detail, covering six different villages, and after selecting 35 households (20% sample) at random, it was found that 100% of the households are in debt. If 7 households are excluded from this list, those who have taken loan from the Banks and Cooperative Societies 28 households or 80% of the total households depend on local money-lenders. Usually the money-lenders advance the amount with 10% interest per month. The inability to repay and eventual accrual of interest compels the Ho to surrender either his small piece of land or the bullocks/goats or the jewelleries of his wife or sister. The incidence of bonded labour, however, was not found, as the Ho somehow manage to get the day's contract as labour either in the mines, factories or with the forest contractors.

Social Tie and Economic Behaviour

Unlike some other neighbouring tribes, the Ho money-lenders are not found, as almost all of them are equally poor. At the time of emergency like sudden illness, house-burning, accident etc., the Ho, when seek for the help of their kinsmen, never return empty-handed. If not in cash, they are helped in kind to meet the emergency.

The social obligation of prestation and gift-giving still continues, which shows that the social relation regulates economic behaviour. Although bride-price is drastically curtailed ,a lot of expenditure is being incurred in marriage feasts, processions etc. All the relatives attend the ceremony with gifts, both in cash and kind, which are highly taxing for them.

CHAPTER FIVE

Traditional Polity and Social Control

The traditional political structure of any community in Mayurbhanj was intimately associated with the contemporary kingship. The king was regarded as the supreme commander of the entire political machinery of the state. Existing documents reveal that for the purpose of politico-administrative control and management, the kings were dividing the state into various units and the attempt was not to spare any individual from the fold of administration.

Written records testify the fact that the kingdom of Mayurbhanj was founded in 598 A.D. Till the merger of the state with greater Orissa, at least three different systems of state administration can be noticed in Mayurbhanj. The earliest structure, which perhaps continued upto 1590 A.D. was a relatively simple one. The king was supported by 22 *sarbarakars* or *dasa rajas*, who were the regional heads. Revenue collection and judiciary was left to them. Every village had similarly a secular leader, *pradhan*, to collect revenue and to help maintaining law and order within his jurisdiction. He was assisted by a *dakua* or messenger. From 1590 A.D. to 1829 A.D., *zamindars* were introduced into the state structure, who were the sub-regional heads to smoothen the process of tax collection. After 1829 A.D., a more elaborate system was introduced by the king Jádunath Bhanja Deo to systematize the state administration. A comparison between the systems can be attempted this way:

Position	*After 1829 A.D.*	*1590-1829 A.D.*	*598-1590 A.D.*
Central Authority	King	King	King
Regional Head	Tehsildar	Sarbarakar	Sarbarakar
Sub-regional Head	Sardar	Zamindar	—
Village Head	Pradhan	Pradhan	Pradhan
Assistant to Village Head	Dakua & Chowkidar	Dakua	Dakua

The King

As pointed out earlier, the king was honoured as the supreme commander of the state. The throne was a hereditary right and primogeniture was the rule of descent, as in other princely states of Orissa. Adoption, however, was common, when there was no heir. Adoption was mostly confined to the neighbouring kingdoms. Widows occupying the throne was not uncommon, when the king was minor.

Although in later times, the king was only concerned with revenue collection, earlier the king had judicial powers. Unsettled disputes at the village and regional levels were being sent to the king for final judgement and his decision was taken to be final. The relationship between the village and regional leaders and the king was maintained in the traditional way, when there was presentation of gifts (*bheti*) during festive occasions by the leaders to the king. The king was also reciprocating by arranging feasts in honour of the leaders, when they visited the royal palace. There are many instances of the Ho and other communities of Mayurbhanj fighting under the leadership of the king against the external enemies.

Sarbarakar

The state of Mayurbhanj was initially divided into various *pirha* or *garha* for better administration, and every *pirha* into *parganas*, and then into many revenue villages. Earlier, every *pirha* or region was under the control of a *sarbarakar*. The Ho of the area still remember the names of five *garhas*, namely, Adipur, Karanjia, Jashipur, Matia and Ratanpur. The post of *sarbarakar* was hereditary. As a regional head, he was getting 50 acres of rent-free land from the king and it was customary to retain 50 per cent of the revenue collected. Before 1803, he was also having judiciary power and was visiting all the villages under his jurisdiction twice in a year for revenue collection and settlement of disputes. In 1829, the *sarbarakar* post was replaced by tehsildars by the king Jadunath Bhanj Deo, who was more radical and progressive in his outlook. The tehsildars were paid employees of the state.

Sardar

The post of *sardar* was first introduced in 1853 in Mayurbhanj. *Sardar* was the revenue head of a *pargana* and was answerable to the tehsildar. He was also having a little judicial power, but the major cases were left to the police, which had started functioning by that time. The post of *sardar* was not hereditary and he was nominated by the king. He used to get 20 acres of rent-free land as his remuneration.

Pradhan

The real polity starts with the *pradhan* in a Ho village. Although the *pradhan* was the agent of the king in the matters of revenue collection and secret messenger of the developments in and around his village, he was the representative of the entire village. The post of *pradhan* was hereditary and the eldest son had the first right of becoming the *pradhan* at the death or retirement of his father. In case of death or incapability of the first son, the second son becomes the *pradhan* of the village. Although no definite qualification was prescriptive for the selection of *pradhan*, in normal cases, the head of the numerically dominant clan was unanimously selected for the post. However, dynamism and integrity of the individual were taken into consideration for the selection. Women were debarred from this opportunity.

The *pradhan* used to get 10 per cent of the total revenue collection from his village and 15 acres of rent-free land from the king as his remuneration. But most of the times he had to deposit the land tax on behalf of some poor and incapable villagers, to whom he represented and was to share all the matters—

joys and sorrows. There was no remuneration from the village for his responsibilities as *pradhan*, excepting the honour that was given to him by all the villagers. However, he was not to give any direct payment to the villagers when they work in his fields. But providing with the mid-day meal to all those workers was compulsory.

Powers and Functions

Traditionally, the *pradhan* was the representative of the entire village both in external and internal matters. He was the head of the village judiciary, supported by the village elders. His decision was regarded as final and the parties had to abide by his decisions. Usually the cases of land disputes, sexual violence, intra and inter-family quarrels, theft, encroachment, inheritance, divorce disputes etc. were being decided by the *pradhan* and justice was given to the deserving individuals of the village. In case of a complaint to those effects, the *pradhan* used to convene a meeting on an appointed evening. The *dakua* had the responsibility of informing all the villagers the date and time of meeting. When the villagers had assembled, the parties had to narrate their arguments and counter-arguments. On the basis of that and with the consultation of the elders, the *pradhan* was to convey his decision, which was binding to both the parties concerned.

The executive power was also vested with the *pradhan*. Although there was hardly any case of disobedience to the orders, in such a case, he was to take stern action by way of ostracism or heavy penalty etc. mainly to keep the law and order maintained in the community.

Another power of the *pradhan*, as mentioned earlier, was to collect land tax (rajaya) on behalf of the king of Mayurbhanj. Even after Indian independence, for some time, the *pradhan* was collecting land tax for which he was given monthly salary. Traditionally, however, he was collecting land tax (rajaya), fruit tax (janajaya), road tax (hararajaya), water tax (darajaya) etc. twice in a year, in the months of *pousha* (December-January) and *falguna* (February-March) after the harvest. He was to deposit the revenue at the state treasury or with the *sardar*. Although the *pradhan* was coming to the rescue of some genuinely needy villagers by depositing their taxes, if an individual was found to be defaulter for four consecutive years, he had to allot the land to some other individuals or to report to the *sardar* and *sarbarakar* for necessary action. Since most of them were illiterate but had to keep records of all the revenue collection, some literate persons were appointed to assist the *pradhan* in these respects. They were getting Rs. 3 as monthly salary and 2 acres of rent-free land.

Besides the role of a *pradhan* as the secular head of the village, he had also some roles to play in communal and domestic rituals. No communal festival could be performed without his presence or consent. In fact, he used to instruct the *dehuri* for the selection of an auspicious date for communal festival. In some cases he had to initially offer animal sacrifice to the deity and was getting the head of the sacrificed animal as his share. In general, he used to preside over the communal festivals. In domestic rituals also he was invited In marriage negotiations particularly, the village *pradhan* had a significant role to play as the chief mediator. His role in divorce and remarriage was also not less important as mediator.

Further, the *pradhan* was responsible for arranging *bethi* or free labour for the king, *sarbarakar* or for the general well-being of the state like road construction, temple making etc.

Dakua

This was the post of a messenger and was to assist the village headman in all possible ways. The post was also hereditary. But the loyalty to the *pradhan* mattered much for the continuation of the post. There was no prescribed qualification for the post excepting the general moral conduct of the individual. The post *dakua* used to get Rs. 3 as his monthly remuneration and 2 acres of rent-free land from the king. Once he quitted the post, he had to surrender the land. Besides that, the villagers used to give him one bundle of paddy per family and other harvested items like pulses, oilseeds etc.

The function of a *dakua* was mainly to assist the headman. He was carrying the message of the date of tax collection, visit of king or high officials, orders for free labour, auction sale of land in case of non-payment of taxes etc. Besides all these, he used to carry the message of village meetings to individual families. Further, the *pradhan* had to send him to the state capital, regional head's office or to other villages in connection with the village or extra village matters. The *dakua* was highly honoured in the village as a royal agent.

Chowkidar

The post of *chowkidar* was introduced in Mayurbhanj in the year 1894 to inform the cases of birth, death, suicide etc. to the state police. He was appointed by the *sardar* in consultation with the village *pradhan*. He used to get a monthly remuneration of Rs. 3 only. He was also to assist the police in criminal investigations and to *pradhan* during revenue collection. He was the watchman of the village and was responsible for security of the village. His turban and stick was giving an appearance of a true loyal agent on duty. His respect in the village was in no way less. His appointment was cancelled in case of misconduct or negligence in duties by the *sardar* on the recommendation of the village headman.

The political structure in the villages of Mayurbhanj in general and that of any Ho village in particular was directly connected with kingship. The leadership of the king was thought to be charismatic and his orders were carried out unhesitatingly by a Ho citizen unassumingly, even the king's *darshan* in the whole of one's lifetime was not possible.

Social Control

The Ho society recognizes various kinds of negative and ritual sanctions for the violence of social norms. Strict adherence to such sanctions ensures a smoothly functioning Ho society, which is well knit and neatly integrated like many other tribal societies in Orissa and elsewhere.

At the family level, the household head (father in a nuclear family) has the grave responsibility of maintaining peace and integrity in the family. For minor offences like disobedience and other acts that brings in bad name to the family, a member in the family is warned not to repeat the act. But in major offences like violation of incest taboo, theft and other anti-social activities, the family has to abide by the decisions of the village council and punishment upto ostracism may be imposed on the culprit.

At the village level, *pradhan* officiates at all the meetings, concerned with the law and order situations in the village. Most of the cases relate to marriage and violence of sex. Although the Ho society is sexually highly liberal, violation of incest or intra-clan marriage is never tolerated. It is observed that the Ho forcibly forbid the culprits to stay with the village community and eventually, they have to leave for other villages. Public mockery is thought to be highly ridiculous and the offender is treated with ridicule like spitting on the face at a public place. These negative sanctions refrain the individual Ho from indulging in nefarious activities. Witch-craft is always viewed with suspicion and the members engaged in such an offence are penalized with ostracism for the whole life.

Ritual sanctions also help in maintaining social integrity and acting as per the perpetual norms of the society. Crop failure, diseases and death, natural calamities etc. are conceptualized to occur due to the failure in proper propitiation of the ancestors or the *bongas* or Ho gods and goddesses. Any such outbreak culminates in elaborate sacrifice before the *bongas*, both at family and communal levels.

Village and inter-village councils decide the cases of violence in existing norms. The *pradhan* or the *sardar*, with the advice of the village elders declare the nature of punishment. In certain minor offences like quarrel or mis-behaviour, the culprit has to pay for the drinks and a communal feast. Serious offences like murder are handed over the police through the village *chowkidar* immediately.

Inter-village meetings are convened, when major and serious offences are committed by a villager, which involve the neighbouring villages also. Theft from other villages or violation of incest by the individuals of two different villages, eve-teasing to other village women etc. warrant inter-village meetings. In case of inter-ethnic marriages, rendering services to other socially inferior communities like *ghasia* etc. also help initiating an inter-village meeting to decide the nature of punishment. Usually the summon is issued to the concerned village elders under the signatures of the *sardar* and the concerned *pradhans.* On the appointed day and time the proceedings start and the culprit has to obey the punishment as decided in the meeting.

The fear for negative social sanctions keeps the Ho society in check and no socially disapproved acts are encouraged. Although with changing times, most of the cases are handed over to police, the village *pradhan* and the elders still are inclined to settle the minor cases inside the village, which ensures fair justice to the village members and also reinforces the integrity of the village.

CHAPTER VI

Religious Beliefs and Rituals

Like most other communities, the Ho strongly believe in supernatural beings and have faith on the soul of departed individuals. Both gods and goddesses are termed as *bonga* by the Ho, who regulate their day to day individual and communal behaviour. Every *bonga* is feared for, as the slightest deviation in its propitiation may lead to irreparable damage to the entire village by the outbreak of epidemics or crop failure or death by wild animals etc. Ho gods and goddesses are non-anthropomorphic and are believed to hover around hills, forests, cultivated fields within the village premises. Of course, every Ho village has a permanent abode for their *bongas*, which is usually a sal groove (*jatira*), a little away from the village, where regular sacrifice is offered to them. The spirits of dead ancestors normally take shelter inside the single-roomed house, where offerings are made in their honour no festive occasions. Ho *bongas* are divided into two types, such as, the benevolent and the malevolent, depending on their nature. Although no definite hierarchical order of the *bongas* is recognized by these Ho, there is a general consensus that 'sing bonga' is the chief among all, who created the universe.

Sing bonga

'Sing bonga' among the Ho is otherwise called as 'dharam debata' or the sun god. He is believed to be omnipresent and hence, no definite place of worship is accorded to him. He is worshipped first at any festive occasion and the *dehuri* or the village priest sacrifices a white chicken (*sim*) in his honour. Even in family worships, 'sing bonga' is propitiated first and then the other gods or spirits. The Ho even swear in his name to express the truth and during any kind of give and take, with the belief that the god is the only witness for the transactions.

Basuki Thakurani

She is the earth goddess and is worshipped as one of the protectors of the entire Ho community. Her worship, like that of the sing bonga, is done during every ritual and usually a black chicken is offered in her honour. Every Ho, young and old, before taking their delicious drink, rice beer (*diang*), pour a few drops on the earth, which is thought to be an offer to the earth goddess. In household rituals also, 'basuki thakurani' is worshipped before the real ritual begins.

Gram Siri

He is the presiding deity of the village and protects the entire village and its inhabitants. *Gram siri* and his wife *kiasuni thakurani* are represented by two stones decorated with vermilion inside the *jahera* or *bongasal.* The village deity and his consort are also worshipped during every ritual like *Magh Parab, Ba Parab* etc. Red chickens are usually sacrificed in honour of these deities. Any deviation in his propitiation culminates in natural calamities.

Marang Bonga

'Marang Bonga' is the clan deity of the Ho. Every clan or a group of clans has one *marang bonga,* who is thought to be the protector of the respective clan/clans. Any household pooja includes offering to the clan deity and at irregular intervals, the clan members arrange feasts as a token of reverence to their clan deity. Any Ho individual cannot afford to neglect the worship of the clan deity, which causes serious illness and crop failure. A list of some clans and their *marang bonga* are presented below :

1.	Katuburu marang bonga		Chattar, jerai, sinku, pingua, laguri, babanga, chattamba etc.
2.	Samamgandu	,,	tiria, kanakel
3.	Hisichalu	,,	hembram
4.	Disung	,,	purti, tiu etc.
5.	Jirjapat	,,	gagrai
6.	Chhutuburu	,,	samath
7.	Mangalpat	,,	goia
8.	Betarguda	,,	soren

Buru Bonga

This is the deity of the forest for the Ho. In spite of decreasing demand on the forest, the Ho still propitiate the *buru bonga*. During communal ceremonial hunting, after deciding the forest camp, the village *dehuri* offers chicken to the forest god for their success in the venture. Besides communal hunting, before moving to the forest, a group of individuals worship the forest god. They believe that *buru bonga* protects them in the forest and nothing evil happens till the deity is satisfied.

Buddhipat

In Ho pantheon, *Buddhipat* is the goddess, responsible for rainfall. Under the conditions of drought or when there is excessive rainfall, threatening the human habitation, the Ho worship rain goddess. Her abode is not the village sacred groove, but the nearby hill top, where offerings are made by the village *dehuri*.

Dessauli Bonga

Dessauli is the goddess of the diseases according to the Ho belief. She causes great and deadly diseases like small pox, cholera and other epidemics. These diseases are collectively known as *maranghasu* by the Ho, as they do not distinguish individual disease. With the outbreak of epidemics, propitiation starts in honour of *dessauli* by all the villagers headed by the *dehuri*. It is believed that the goddess is provoked and all possible steps are taken to release her anger. The *dessauli* instructs the *dehuri* in dream about all her desire and accordingly sacrifices of chickens, goats etc. are made to cool her down.

The above list of the *bongas* among the Ho is not exhaustive or complete by any standard and is only of a selected few, which are widely recognized among them. One goes on adding to this list while talking with a *dehuri*, who is inclined to add all the spirits like that of a tree, pond, field, river, hillock and so on.

Spirits

As stated earlier, the Ho believe in various types of spirits. According to their cognitive perception, every object—animate or inanimate—has a spirit. In case of human beings, the spirits rest inside their houses after death. The spirits of dead ancestors are believed to be benevolent and these protect not only their descendants, but also the household materials during the absence of the family members. The ancestral spirits are collectively termed as *oagaeka* in Ho language. They rest at the kitchen of the family and are propitiated on each and every festive occasion. When the *dehuri* worships the village deity, the head of the household offers rice-beer and other items to the ancestral spirits.

Religious Functionaries

Every Ho village has a priest, commonly known as *dehuri*, who performs all the worships to different deities on behalf of the villagers. There is no strict rule that the post is exclusively open for the Ho. Even neighbouring communities like the Bathudi take over the priesthood of a Ho village. The post is hereditary. Before his death or voluntary retirement, the priest makes his eldest son proficient in the art of worshipping. The priest may be married or unmarried, but he has to maintain strong morality. Usually, one day before the major communal festivals, he has to abstain from sexual intercourse and has to observe fasting on the day of festival. *Dehuri* is the insignia of village welfare and his only duty is to please the gods and goddesses for maintaining healthy and prosperous life in the village. Before any ritual, he prays to *sing bonga* and *Basu mata* with the following lore :

"Aeham tihinj daham,
Sirmare sing bonga, basukire basmata,
Janamken, jatakenaben, hisiganda dangsi guti hanak ganak,
Lekaka gandakakaben, haraaka, jangiakakaben jahar."

The rough translation of the prayer is, "I am praying before the *sing bonga* and *Basumata* that let them kindly take care of their thousands of children, to whom they procreated."

The post of *dehuri* is remunerative. Some villages have a few decimil of land, earmarked for the priest. In other villages, the priest demands his remuneration in cash or kind. Besides, during every ritual he is offered free rice-beer, paddy, other crops and some money. In no case, a priest is given an opportunity to be displeased or unsatisfied. During certain festivals, where goats and sheep are sacrificed, the priest gets the head of the animal as his share. This custom is repeated in ceremonial huntings also. The overall status of a priest is certainly higher and he is treated with reverence in a Ho village.

The Ho also recognize medicinemen, who are popularly known as *raulia*. Since the Ho believe in spirits and their influence causing diseases, they take the help of *raulia* to diagnose the spirit and necessary propitiation for its satisfaction. The *raulia* uses various methods for the diagnosis and the common one being oil-water method. He collects the urine of the patient and puts a drop of oil on it. If the oil moves on the urine, the disease is simple; if the oil does not move, the disease is due to a spirit. In case of the latter, he advises for propitiation of a particular spirit and then, *dehuri* is called for worship. Sometimes, *raulia* himself chants *mantras* to remove the evil spirit out of the body of the patient.

The post of *raulia,* in most of the cases, is hereditary. The son has to learn all the magical spells by heart from his father or from a teacher. After paying the honorarium of the teacher, he starts functioning independently. There is no fixed remuneration for the medicineman, excepting when he is called for to attend to a patient. He is a well-paid practitioner. Since he mediates between the mundane world and that of the spirits, he is duly cared for by all the villagers and is regarded as an important functionary. There may be a number of such medicinemen in a Ho village, specializing in some diseases. One can come across a *hasu raulia*, *basan-marang hasu raulia* and *sapakati raulia*, specialist in fever, epidemics and snake-bite respectively.

Life-Cycle Rituals

The Ho observe birth, name-giving, marriage and death rituals elaborately and spend lavishly in treating their fellow villagers. Initiation rituals are not observed among them. Puberty ritual is simple.

Birth Rituals

A child is always greeted to a Ho family, who is thought to be an asset. A son, however, is preferred, although a daughter is never neglected or ignored. Barren ladies are regarded as symbols of inauspiciousness and are avoided in Ho society. There are no dietary or other restrictions before and in early months of pregnancy. But when the time of delivery draws nearer, the mother is not allowed to move around the places, where the spirits and *bongas* are suspected to rest. Just before the labour pain starts, all members of the family except the father leave the hut. He helps the wife during delivery, cleans the new-born baby, cuts the umbilical cord and cooks food for first three days. The family remains ceremonially unclean for a month. The mother does not cook for a month and she is not touched by others excepting her husband for first nine days. The mother is given warm rice, dal during these days and fish/meat or rice-beer is strictly forbidden for her. If the family is affluent enough, rice-beer is offered to lineage members on 5th, 9th and 10th days of child birth. This is, however, not compulsory.

Name-giving Rituals

Usually, the new-born baby is named on the 21st day, which is termed as *Numutupuria* by the Ho. The names of maternal or paternal grand parents are preferred. For name giving, an elderly male person of the lineage is invited. He keeps a bowl of water and puts two grains of sun-dried rice in the water while uttering the name of a grand parent. If the grains get united at the bottom of the bowl, the name is believed to be auspicious for the child and accepted. If not, a new name is suggested. The trial and error method continues, till a name is selected. The genealogy on page 55 reflects that names are repetitive in Ho society.

On the day of *Numutupuria*, the child is nicely bathed in warm water. All the used clothes are cleaned. The father gets shaved. A feast is arranged, depending on the economic condition of the family. Rice, meat and rice-beer are enjoyed by all the members of the lineage.

Puberty Rituals

No definite ceremony is associated with the onset of first menstrual cycle of a girl. The age of first menstruation among the Ho varies from ten to twelve years. During this, the girl remains aloof for a period of seven days and lives in a separate room, if possible. They have a belief that if the girl during these seven days touches a boy, he becomes bloodless and ultimately dies. On the seventh day, she smears her body with turmeric paste and takes bath. Then she leads a normal life. If the first menstruation falls on a Tuesday, Thursday or Sunday, the Ho feel it highly inauspicious and there is a belief that the marriage of the girl will not be smooth and normal. In such a situation, the girl's father arranges for worship and sacrifice to *Sing Bonga* at the advice of the village *dehuri*.

Marriage (Andi)

Marriage ritual is highly expensive for both the families of the bride and the groom. The bride-price is very high among the Ho, which has culminated in a considerable percentage of spinsters in their society. Monogamous marriage is most preferred and clan exogamy is strictly followed in Ho society. Preferential cross-cousin marriages are widely observed and secondary marriages like levirate, sorrorate and widow

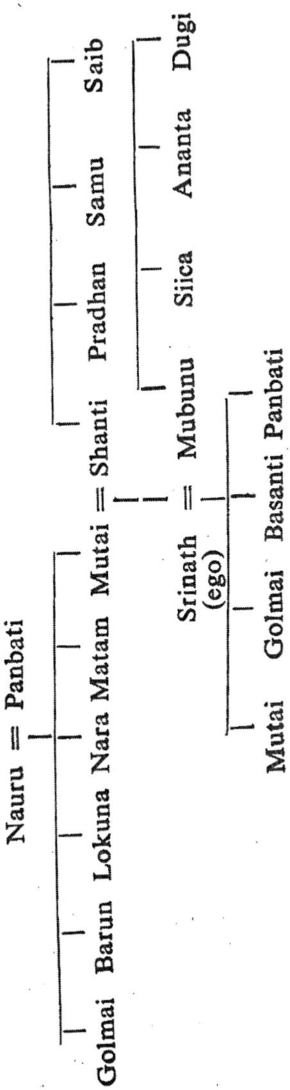
Nauru = Panbati
Golmai
Barun
Lokuna
Nara
Matam
Mutai = Shanti
Pradhan
Samu
Saib
Srinath
(ego)
= Mubunu
Siica
Ananta
Dugi
Mutai
Golmai
Basanti
Panbati

remarriage are practised. The following modes of acquiring mates are common :

1. Marriage by negotiation	Abua sukute andi or Diku andi
2. Marriage by capture	Opertipi andi
3. Marriage by elopement	Raji khusi andi
4. Marriage by intrusion	Anader andi
5. Marriage by adoption	Gardi jamai andi
6. Marriage by exchange	Badal andi

Excepting *diku andi*, all forms of marriage are arranged at the groom's residence. For marriage by negotiation, a mediator, preferably the headman of the groom's village becomes necessary to pursue with the marriage formalities. The mediator first approaches the bride's father and preliminary discussions on bride-price take place. Then on an appointed day, the groom and his relatives visit the bride's village. They carry with them rice, dal, he-goats, rice-beer and other requirements. In the bride's residence, the groom offers rice-beer in a sal leaf-cup to the bride. If she accepts, the marriage consent is symbolically given. The groom's party prepare their food and in the evening they sing and dance with the girls of the village. The next morning they return back. Similarly a party of the bride's relatives, unaccompanied by the bride, pay a visit to the groom's village. After the bride-price is agreed upon by both the parties, a date is fixed for marriage with the consent of the village *dehuri*. Usually, marriages are solemnized during the post-harvest months.

On the morning of the day fixed for the ceremony, some members of the groom's family proceed towards the bride's village with rice-beer and presents to escort the bride. In the afternoon they escort the bride, accompanied by the bride's relatives. When they approach the groom's village, at the outskirt, a mock fight begins between both the parties. After this, the bride is greeted to the house. A pandal is erected for this purpose in the courtyard of the groom's house. In the evening, both the groom and the bride sit on the pandal. Rice is cooked on the spot in a new earthen pot. The *dehuri* worships the *Sing Bonga* and other gods. Both the groom and the bride touch the cooked rice, meant for offering to ancestral spirits, which brings in the bride to the clan of the groom. The marriage ritual ends with giving vermilion to the bride by her new husband and feasting and dancing follow throughout the night.

Death Rituals

The death ritual is elaborate among the Ho. As soon as a member passes away, message is sent to all the relatives. The dead body (*gayana*) is then prepared for cremation. A stretcher is prepared for this purpose. The corpse is anointed with oil, turmeric paste; shaved and washed off neatly. New cloth is wrapped on the dead body. The ornaments and utensils of the individual are kept near him. Before taking the corpse for cremation, seeds are put under the head of the corpse with the belief that these seeds can procure better harvest. The male members of the village carry the corpse and the procession to the graveyard is accompanied by the females as well.

Every clan has a definite cremation ground. The corpse is carried to the ground and the pyre (*Jalpamutu*) is prepared. After the pyre is lit, the body is placed on it with the head towards south and face upwards in fully stretched position. The next day, bones of the deceased are collected by the sons or the close relatives and put in a new earthen pot for final purification rite at the nearby river.

The mourning period continues for 9 days. All the relatives visit the bereaved family with provisions like rice, dal, vegetables and rice-beer. Non-vegetarian food is not taken during this period nor clothes are cleaned with soap. All used earthen cooking utensils are abandoned and new ones are replaced on the 10th day. On the same day, the family members get shaved and find a suitable place for burying the bone of the dead ancestor. A large stone slab is put on the grave as a memory of the departed soul. All clan members and relatives are offered a feast and rice-beer.

On the 10th night (*sapsi*), the kins and relatives invite the departed soul (*ambal*) to the house and live with them. The eldest son in the presence of others soberly utters :

> "A babu ejume ala,
> Ejume abu oate,
> Chimini baharem taina,
> Sikiko hua miia oate ejume."

which means, "Oh father ! come into our house, otherwise mosquitos will bite you and cause trouble for you. For how many days you live outside the house ? Please come in." With the utterance of this time and again, they see the shadow of the departed soul entering into the kitchen and stop chanting further. After the mourning period (*kaman ghar*) is over, the relatives take leave and the family resumes its normal work.

Annual Ritual Cycle

The religious sentiment and devotion to the *bongas* among the Ho culminate in a number of communal festivals, besides the domestic rituals. The Ho observe four major festivals which are communal in nature, and are combinations of socio-religious and recreational activities. These are : (a) Magh pudi, (b) Ba parab, (c) Hera parab, and (d) Jamnam parab.

(a) *Magh pudi* : After the harvest, when the granaries are almost full, the Ho observe this festival during the month of Magha (January-February). The date is fixed in a joint meeting of the *dehuri* and elder members of the village. *Gram siri, Sing Bonga, Buddhipat* and other deities are propitiated for the prosperity of the village. The festival is continued for six days and invariably followed by drinking and dancing, which facilitates choosing marital partners among the youth. These six days of celebration are named separately by the Ho :

1st day	gawal
2nd day	ate ili
3rd day	sange ili
4th day	marang-musing
5th day	basi-musing
6th day	har bagia

On the first day of the festival (gawal), there is no communal worship excepting that every household offers pooja to the ancestral spirits. Rice-beer is prepared for the purpose and ceremonial offering of rice, curry and rice-beer is made to the spirits. All members of the household, irrespective of age and sex, drink the rice-beer in the night. The house is cleaned with cow-dung water on this day.

The second day is the offering of ili or rice-beer to the *bongas* by the village priest. Every household head assembles at the residence of the *dehuri* with a pot of rice-beer. After the formal offering of rice-beer is made to the *bongas*, the villagers drink rice-beer as much as they can and dance.

On the third day, again the villagers wash their houses clean. The courtyard, granaries etc. are cleaned with cow-dung water. Even this solution is sprinkled over all the used materials like utensils. The people of the village do not attend to any work except drinking, dining and dancing.

The fourth day marks the real ritual part of the festival. A pandal is specially erected for the purpose outside the village. The pandal is decorated by the village youth. The priest along with the villagers comes to the pandal around the mid-day. The villagers bring a big pot of rice-beer. Chickens are procured for the purpose. The priest scatters sun-dried rice. It is regarded as auspicious, if the chickens swallow them. Then the sacrifice of these chickens is made to *dessauli, gram siri, sing bonga* etc. to protect the village. After the propitiation is over, the villagers, male and female, drink rice-beer and dance with obscene songs, narrating the male and female organs or inviting each other for sexual intercourse.

The fifth day is the day of bidding good-bye to the invited spirits. The village youth sing and dance. On the sixth day, they beat the roof of every house in a group with the belief that this act expels all diseases, miseries from the village and brings in peace. They collect rice, vegetables etc. from every household and arrange a feast outside the village.

The festival is unavoidable for any Ho village and any

deviation to the observance invites only miseries to the villagers. In spite of this folk belief, the festival is otherwise thought to be recreational and smoothens the process of selecting life partners.

(b) *Ba Parab* : This festival is also termed as *Phulbhanguni,* which is observed in the month of Chaitra (February-March). The Ho have the new fruits like mango, jack-fruit and mohua and sal flowers are to be offered to the deities, before these are taken by the villagers. The festival stretches over a period of four days.

On the first day (*he sakam diang*), the villagers move to the forest. The female members collect sal leaves, while the males seek for a hunt. Towards mid-day all return back to their respective houses and worship the ancestral spirits. Drinking rice-beer and dancing in the evening mark the occasion.

The second day (*marang musing*) is the day of actual ritual. During *magh pudi,* the *dehuri* sacrifices chickens and he-goats with chanting of mantras in honour of *dessauli, gram siri, sing bonga* etc. After ceremonial offering of sal and mohua flowers, the priest distributes them among the villagers. Then, drinking and dancing begins. Meat and rice are prepared and a feast is arranged in the same afternoon.

The third day (*basi musing*) and fourth day (*bala badni*) are meant for the expulsion of the invited spirits. On the third day, ancestral spirits are worshipped, while the next day a feast is arranged by all the villagers. Dancing and singing constitute a major part of the festival.

(c) *Hera Parab* : This ritual is essentially related to the agricultural cycle of the Ho, who conventionally profess agriculture. As this a communal festival, even the landless of the village participate in the ritual. *Dehuri,* in consultation with the villagers, fixes a date in the month of Baisakh (March-April) for this festival, which is celebrated as the first sowing festival. The ritual continues for a period of three days. The first day is only preparatory like cleaning the houses, collection of sal leaves for ritual purpose etc. In subsequent two days, all the villagers participate in the propitiation of *gram siri* and *kiasuni thakurani* for better harvest. On the second day usual sacrifices of chickens in the *gramsal* are made by *dehuri* and drinking and dancing begin in the evening. On the third day, the *dehuri*, after worshipping the deities, starts sowing paddy in his fied. He is followed by the female members of the society, who ceremonially sow some seed in a corner of their respective fields. This festival is for better harvest. It is not celebrated as lavishly as the other two festivals, precisely because the granaries become nearly empty by the time the ritual falls.

(d) *Jamnam Parab* : This festival is also known as *nuakhia parab* and is celebrated during the month of Aswina (October-November). As the name of the festival implies, it is intended for the first consumption of rice after harvest. Even they harvest paddy much before, it is not taken until this community festival is finished. The date is fixed as per the convenience of the villagers. On the appointed day, the priest worships the *gram siri, kiasuni thakurani* and other deities. People give new rice for offering to the deities and the returned part is ceremonially cooked and eaten by family members. As usual, the festival is followed by drinking and dancing throughout the night.

Besides these major festivals, the Ho also observe *Padistha Dibasa* (foundation day of village), *Makar Parab, Ashadhi Parab, Gamha Parab* etc. The celebration of the festivals clearly reveals the religious stigma attached to the Ho social life, who spend lavishly on these occasions, in spite of the state of poverty they commonly encounter.

CHAPTER SEVEN

Development Efforts and Effects

Immediately after independence, one of the major objectives of the Government of India was to take up the programmes for the development of the weaker sections and economically backward communities in the country. Exclusively for the tribal areas and the tribal people development programmes are launched with a two-fold objective. The first objective is area development and the second is for the economic uplift of individual tribal beneficiaries. Area development contemplates mainly on the development of infrastructure in the tribal areas through the expansion of irrigation, communication, medical facilities, promotion of education including the non-formal, development of horticulture, provision of soil conservation measures, rural electrification and provision of drinking water facilities etc. Economic upliftment of individual tribal families is sought to be achieved by providing various income generating schemes for the tribals under ITDA, IRDP, ERRP, supplemented by Special Central Assistance and various sectors of the State Plan.

There have been many concerted efforts for the overall development of the tribal population by the Government from time to time. The tribal sub-plan has been formulated and being implemented since the beginning of the 5th Five Year Plan as an effective instrument for tribal development. Quantification of funds from different sources for the sub-plan area, and fixation of physical targets to be achieved under different sectoral programmes for speedier development of the tribal areas and the life-styles of the tribals are the characteristic features of the tribal sub-plan approach.

Area and Population

Orissa has a special place in the tribal map of India, which has as many as 62 Scheduled Tribes, constituting about 22.43 per cent of the total State population, as per 1981 census. The tribal sub-plan area in Orissa covers 118 Community Development Blocks out of a total of 314 in the State. The area covered by the tribal sub-plan is about 69,490 sq. kms., constituting approximately 44.6 per cent of the total area of the State.

The total population of the State as per 1981 census is 2,63,70,217. But as per 1971 figures, the total population in the sub-plan area was 61,20,239, thus constituting 27.90 per cent of the total State population in 1971. The total tribal population of the State according to 1981 census was 59,15,067 and the total tribal population coming under the sub-plan area was 40,01,025, constituting about 67.64 per cent of the total tribal population in the State.

In order to give operational effect to the sub-plan approach, 21 ITDAs have been constituted in the State, out of which the areas of 19 ITDAs are coterminus with that of the concerned revenue sub-divisions. A comprehensive plan is formulated for each of the ITDAs and the sectoral programmes of development are monitored at both district and state levels.

Micro Projects

Besides the operation of tribal sub-plan, a special scheme is implemented for the extremely backward tribal groups or 'primitive tribes' since the 5th Five Year Plan, which is known as special Micro Projects. The primitive tribes are identified, following the norms fixed by the Planning Commission and Government of India. The basic norms are—(1) pre-agricultural level of technology, (2) low level of literacy, and (3) stagnant or diminishing population. On the basis of these norms, 12 tribal communities have so far been identified in the State of Orissa, and special micro projects are in operation among them. The major objective of the project is to develop a sense of awareness among the tribes about various developmental efforts, and to initiate them in the process of being benefited out of the above efforts. It is rather a way to bring development to the doorsteps of the backward tribal population.

Due to, perhaps, their practice of settled agriculture and associated with the process of industrialization in the State, the Ho do not come under the category of primitive tribes. Therefore, they are not covered under a micro project. But they elicit whatever benefit available from various Government plans and programmes through different development agencies like the Block, LAMPS, commercial banks, P.H.C. etc. With a view to note the development programmes and the association of the Ho in them, one block, Jashipur in the district of Mayurbhanj has been selected, where the Ho are numerically dominant. This block is a representative of the rest other community development blocks in the Ho area of the district in Orissa.

Block as an Agent of Development

Jashipur block in the district of Mayurbhanj was constituted on 1st April, 1959 and was converted to a Community Development block on 1st April, 1960. Again on 1st April, 1966, it was declared as a tribal development block, as more than 60 per cent of the population was formed by the tribals. There are 13 Gram Panchayats under Jashipur block and 224 villages in total. As per 1971 census, the total population of Jashipur block was 62,650, out of which 42,092 were tribals. The total area coverage of the block is 22,48,604 hectares. The block normally undertakes the following developmental programmes for the local inhabitants including the Ho population.

Drinking Water Facilities

Dug well facility is extended to the villagers to meet the demand of drinking water and to dissuade them to use the unhygienic water of the streams, ponds or nallahs for the purpose of drinking. The ITDA finances for the dug wells, basing on the recommendations of the block. During 1978-79, 35 dug well schemes were undertaken by Jashipur block for the benefit of the tribals. But it is often observed that the dug wells are not very much appreciated by the Ho. The factors are many. Distance of the well from the settlement, lack of water in the summer months, inadequate maintenance and sometimes supernatural beliefs are responsible for abandoning the use of the well temporarily or permanently. Only in a few particular cases, the wells are used continuously.

Educational Facilities

There are 88 schools of different types, running under Jashipur block. Besides grants sanctioned for construction and repair of school buildings, the tribal students upto Class V are given reading and writing materials. These are given free of cost. Stipends are also given to high school students and post-matric scholarships to the college students for development of their educational standards. There are also some *sevashrama* schools, which are meant for the tribal students and are residential in nature.

Adult education programme for the benefit of the adult non-literate tribals above 15 years of age has been introduced in Jashipur block since 1980. During 1980, 150 candidates were trained as teachers, and the training programme was financed by the C.D. department of the Government and the ITDA. The expenses incurred for adult education are also met by the Government. Consequent upon the introduction of these development schemes, education has become popular among the Ho and the rate of literacy has gone up considerably among them.

Special Nutrition Programme

Education is supplemented by the nutrition programme in this block. Nutrition programme is of special attraction for the tribal children. With the supplies of wheat, soyabean oil, milk powder etc. by the Government and CARE organization, mid-day meals are prepared for the L.P. and U.P. school children. This is highly alluring for the Ho school-going children as well. This programme does not only bring them to the school, but also helps in providing nutritious diet.

Special Feeding Programme

Special feeding programme is aimed at supplying nutritious diet to the children below five years of age and the expectant mothers. Wheat and soyabean are supplied to the local Mahila Samitis through the block for distribution among the pregnant women and small children every day except Sundays. The Ho women participate in this endeavour only, and they are not serious about other developmental activities of the Mahila Samitis.

Antodaya Scheme

The antodaya scheme started in 1978 and is financed by the ITDA. It is formulated to elevate the economic condition of the poorest among the poor. It is a loan with 50 per cent subsidy and for ensuring an income base for the loanee. Till 1980, 93 families are benefited by this scheme under Jashipur block, out of which 15 families belong to the Ho community. The loan is not given in cash and the loanee is provided with the materials like bicycle, sewing machine, live-stock etc., which would return back the loanee some regular income.

Village Reconstruction Scheme

Sometimes the villagers are affected by the flood in the river, Khairi-Bhandan, flowing near Jashipur. In order to rehabilitate them, a colony of 25 houses has been constructed near Ramtirtha, out of which there are 6 Ho households. They are also given some interim relief.

Old Age Pension Scheme

The scheme is meant for the old, disabled people, not having any source of income. On the recommendations of the local Sarpanch and the B.D.O., pension at the monthly rate of Rs. 25 is being given to many old people. There are some Ho beneficiaries of this scheme as well in Jashipur block.

Construction and Repair of Roads

The construction and repair of roads come under the purview of the block. Jashipur block has extended communication facilities to the villages that come under it within the limited funds available. To villages like Junai and Etamundi there is no all-weather communication facility and efforts are being made to connect them soon. The village roads are constructed by the respective Gram Panchayats and necessary sanctions are made for the purpose. Easy communication has made the Ho mobile and helps them to get exposed to the world outside.

LAMPS as an Agent of Development

Apart from the legal measures against exploitation of the non-tribal money-lenders, the Government has extended cooperative facilities in most of the tribal areas through the tribal blocks. Jashipur block has four branches of Large Sized Multipurpose Cooperative Society (LAMPS) in Jashipur, Bansanali, Matiagarh and Rugudi with a view to providing cheap credit facilities, in cash and in kind, to the needy tribals.

Besides supplying ration cards for purchasing rice, wheat, sugar and kerosene oil at a reasonable rate, LAMPS offers loans to the tribals with 50 per cent subsidy and interest at the rate of 11 per cent per annum. Subsidy is only given to small and marginal farmers, possessing below 5 acres and below 10 acres of non-irrigated land respectively. One year short-term loans for agricultural operation, medium term loan for live-stock etc. repayable within 3 years, and long-term loan for tube-well, pump sets etc. repayable within 7 years are offered to the people. The defaulter has to pay interest at the rate of 2 per cent per annum till he repays the loan amount and interest accrued out of it.

The loan provision of the LAMPS and particularly, the loan of seeds, fertilizers etc. with an amount of subsidy has become very popular among the Ho. It has been often found that they go for it with much interest. But after the harvest, they find it difficult to repay the loan, due to their commitment to the local money-lender to first repay his earlier loan. Very often, they become defaulters, and hence, are not eligible for subsequent loans. Only a section of the Ho, who are a little educated and well off make full utilization of the services offered by the LAMPS.

The linking of credit with marketing through the LAMPS

has not started in Jashipur block till the end of our fieldwork. In future, the scheme would be hopefully popular among the Ho.

Bank as an Agent of Development

The role of a commercial bank is undoubtedly pivotal these days for development. In fact, banks are mutual aid associations whose function is to provide credit on personal security or on the basis of nominal security to its members who are either cultivators, artisans, small or big industrialists. A branch of the Bank of India started in Jashipur in 1973 to cater to the needs of the surrounding tribal population. The bank provides loans to the tribal farmers or entrepreneurs in collusion with the ITDA. The tribals possessing below 10 acres of land are eligible for a bank loan to improve agriculture or other business with 50 per cent subsidy and an interest at the rate of 4 per cent per annum. The subsidy is provided by the ITDA.

Loan from the bank is offered for various purposes to the tribal population. Improvement of agriculture, goattery, piggery, sheep rearing, broilers farm, purchase of bullock, carpentry, tea stall, small grocery shop, basket making, vegetable vending and a variety of other practices come under this. The choice is often of the loanee. But it is found that the Ho normally apply for agricultural loan, and in very rare cases for goattery or purchase of bullocks etc. Still more awareness is essential for them to utilize their loan in many other profitable sectors.

Land Development Bank

In Jashipur, there is an office of land development bank, headed by a supervisor. The bank provides kind or cash loan for agricultural purposes and long-term cashl oan for dug well, tractor, pump set, development of bamboo and *bobai* grass etc. 50 per cent subsidy is granted to the tribal loanees by the bank. The interest charged is at the rate of 9.5 per cent per annum. Here also, the agriculture loan is very popular among the Ho, and loans for other purposes are taken occasionally.

Department of Agriculture as an Agent of Development

After the separation of the department of agriculture from the community development blocks, the department has taken up many new schemes for the benefit of the tribal farmers. Since the Ho are basically settled agriculturists, some of them take advantage of the programmes for a better harvest. The objectives of the department are to introduce new crops, high yielding varieties, modern agricultural implements, use of fertilizers, pesticides, and convince the cultivator to take up advanced agricultural technologies.

The activities of the agriculture department are geared by the V.A.W. or Village Agriculture Worker. One V.A.W. is incharge of 8 units of population, each unit containing 500 to 800 people. At the interval of every 15 days, the V.A.W. visits the unit and guides the farmers to fulfil the objectives of the department. The V.A.W. selects some contact farmers and makes it a point to meet them during his visit to the village.

The Department of Agriculture extends loan facility to the farmers, finances for dug well, minor irrigation programmes, lift irrigation, horticulture and in situ plantation programmes etc. The funds are available for the purpose from the ITDA, through Central assistance and from the Government of Orissa. The Ho find the programmes very effective and accept them. But the major handicap lies at the lack of irrigation facilities in the block. Whatever irrigation programmes are implemented, seem to be inadequate, and interestingly, the individual Ho farmers do not take risk of having their own lift irrigation points. There is an ideal farm near Jashipur, managed by the Orissa University of Agriculture and Technology, which influences the Ho farmers to a great extent.

Social Forestry

The scheme started in Jashipur block in 1976 with the financial assistance of SIDA, and the work being executed by the Forest Department of the Government of Orissa. The operation and management of the scheme has been responsible in the emergence of an awareness among the Ho to protect and develop forest resources for their self-benefit.

Primary Health Centre

The Primary Health Centre (P.H.C.) provides personal health services to all, particularly to mothers and children, school-going children, control of epidemics, family planning, vaccination and health education to the public. The P.H.C. at Jankeswar started in 1964, covering 444 sq. kms. area and a population of 70,268 as per 1971 census. The P.H.C. is divided into three major sections like Public health, Family welfare and Malaria eradication. The P.H.C. extends specialist services in various branches of medicine and surgery. It also has health assistants and supervisors for vaccination programmes, mobile health unit, rural family welfare sub-centre, lady health visitors etc. to make available the health facilities to the individuals at their houses more effectively. There are also two Ayurvedic dispensaries at Ektali and Hajanir to supplement the activities of the P.H.C.

The family welfare programme is being implemented through family planning sub-centres. Every sub-centre has at-least one Auxiliary Nurse Midwife, assisted by some local dais. The local dais are trained for one month by the P.H.C. health visitor and get Rs. 300 as their monthly remuneration, after they are appointed in villages.

Although the health workers move around the villages, the Ho do not show much interest in either vaccination or family welfare programmes. They have the belief that children are potential assets and if they are more in number, there would be more prosperity. This belief is however gradually changing. Although there is no data available with regard to the Ho members sterilized, there is a general figure made available by the P.H.C., Jankeswar about the total number of people sterilized :

Year of Sterilization	*Number of Cases*
1975	152
1976	1516
1977	152
1978	112
1979	280

Veterinary Dispensary

The Veterinary Dispensary started at Jashipur in 1961, and before that, it was functioning as a stock man centre. The dispensary does not only cater to the health needs of the live-stock in the area, but also extends vaccination, artificial insemination and live-stock health education programmes. The Veterinary Surgeon plays a significant role in extension programmes as well, besides his routine duties. The live-stock purchase is always done through the V.A.S. and with his recommendations for the live-stock loanees, the loans being sanctioned by the ITDA. Although the Ho realize that the cattle are their assets, they do not take enough care of them. They bank upon the local medicinemen for any disease of the cattle and do not come to the veterinary dispensary for their treatment.

Effects of Development

One cannot deny the fact that the benefits of the development programmes are made available, in the Ho area, with the endeavour and interest of the officials. But surprisingly, an adequate awareness has not yet developed among the Ho to make use of these programmes in their interest. It is not true also that all the Ho have rejected or not availed of the developmental benefits. There are a few progressive individuals among them, those who take the advantage, and the bulk of the population remain in darkness. This creates a dichotomy in their society with some progressives at the helm of the affairs and most others as a deprived lot. Prevalence of suspicion on the officials and strong belief in superstition make them deprived of the benefits. But with the expansion of education among them, it is believed, future would be hopeful for every individual Ho to make full utilization of the Government helps and become prosperous.

CHAPTER EIGHT

The Ho Society : Then and Now

Change is, perhaps, inevitable for any society at any point of time and at any place; hence, the human society is being rightly characterized by many as the changing units. But usually, while the internal or endogenous changes take a long span of time to get exposed, the external or exogenous changes become too soon apparent to draw the immediate attention of an observer. Besides its many adaptive changes, the Ho society was exposed to the vagaries of modern forces of industrialization long before independence unlike many other tribes of Orissa, and the marks of change in various aspects of their life, society and culture can easily be noticed. Fortunately for us, we have the monographic accounts of the tribe since the late 19th century till recently by many administrators and anthropologists, notable among them being that of by Dalton (1872), Russel and Hiralal (1975), Griffiths (1946), Chatterjee and Das (1927), Majumdar (1955) and a large collection of scientific papers on various aspects of Ho society and culture, which help as chief supports to draw a comparison at different time periods and note the resulting changes. The preceding accounts however are with reference to the section of the tribe, inhabiting the Bihar plateau (Kolhan region) and the Central India, including parts of Maharashtra. But this does not deter us in comparing the conventions of the Kolhan Ho and the Mayurbhanj Ho, which end up with a conclusion that a remarkable contrast is hard to conceive in their respective socio-cultural life. Further, the present investigation confirms the fact that the Ho in Mayurbhanj still attach emotional link with the Ho of Bihar and regard Kolhan as their place of origin.

Changing Social Institution : *The Family*

Forces of industrialization and subsequent urbanization greatly affect the structure and function of the family in the developing world, and the Ho are no exception to this trend. Chatterjee and Das (1927 : 48) note the predominance of joint families among the Ho. But our recent survey indicates that more than 70 per cent of the families among them are nuclear. This change in the structure of the family affects the inter-personal relations as well. Although cordiality and mutual love still bind the siblings and the parent children, the extension of this sentiment is hardly noticed to the members of the kinsmen belonging to the third degree or more. Besides, the number and proportion of broken families are on the increase. The conventional functions of the family as the socializing and security agent are found to be gradually declining. In general, it may be pointed out that atomistic tendency pervades the entire family life these days. The situation is still worse in the villages located either at the urban fringe or at the heart of an industrial-mining location. The probable reasons for such a family disruption include growing self-centrism, alienation from community and wage earning by both husband and wife, which leave little scope for child care and upbringing.

The Marriage

The excess of bride wealth and the eventual higher percentage of spinsterhood among the Ho had drawn the attention of Majumdar (1926 : 150) and even there are evidences of the British administration interfering in this indigenous custom to bring about a compromise for a reasonable bride wealth and to remove this traditional bottleneck from the Ho social structure. The situation is found to have improved during these sixty years, although the convention still perpetuates. These days also, during the post harvest month the Ho arrange the marriage festivals with filled granaries and lavishly spend in dining and drinking.

Modern impact of industrialization by way of free mixing of the young members as co-workers either in mines or factories, has reduced the marriage hazards to a great extent. *Raji khusi andi* (marriage by love and elopement) has become a common scene under the prevailing state with post-marital approval of the parents. The clan exogamy, however, is still honoured and an exception to this has not been reported during the present survey. The impact of neighbouring Hindu caste communities has also immensely influenced the Ho and there are many instances of *diku andi* (marriage by negotiation), which is thought to be more fashionable and prestigious. This new custom no doubt helps reducing the quantum of bride wealth, but warrants heavy expenditure through marriage procession, light, crackers and sumptuous dinner for the invitees. Although these impacts have removed some of the prevailing social evils, there was rise in the flexibility of marital ties. The rate of divorce has now gone up considerably, ending up with many broken families among the Ho of Mayurbhanj.

Kin Ties and Obligations

Changing family relations have often influenced kinship ties and obligations. Gradual transformation of families to atomistic ones and perpetual alienation from the close kinsmen make the child to conceptualize his social universe not much beyond his parents. It has been observed that even kin terms are changed to a great extent due to the influence of the neighbouring communities in an urban-industrial setting. Kinship usages and their respective roles in maintaining balanced and coherent relations are not perhaps found to be as much in operation as those were, when there was a unitary village life.

An important and interesting development, however, in the mining and industrial huttings (colonies) is the organization of a village life with multi-ethnic composition and unusual extension of kin relations beyond the Ho ethnic boundary. This essentially includes huge instances of ritual kinship and ritual friendship. Although this does not undermine the traditional feeling of ethnic distinction, it helps in a big way to create a new communal life, away from one's own community.

Changing Ho Economy

There is mention about the changing occupation and means of subsistence among the Ho in the body of this report (vide chapter IV). It is mentioned that about 51.5% of the total workers are engaged as daily labourers in various mines and industries. This has partially jeopardized the traditional agricultural economy of the Ho. It is beyond any doubt that the per capita income among them has gone up considerably due to wage labour, but this has otherwise affected the agriculturally based coherent village life. Agricultural operation was instrumental in reinforcing integrity among the members of the lineage/clan/village, and mutual sharing of responsibilities was common. But wage earning has made them more self-centric and the bond of emotional attachment is gradually declining, which was hitherto considered as one of the significant criteria of any homogeneous community.

Growing acceptance and internalization of money economy has substituted the traditional mechnanism of exchange. Cash transaction now pervades almost the entire economic scene of the Ho life. This trend, coupled with the profuse extension of market network, have exposed them mercilessly to the vagaries of modern forces of change. Gradual increase in the use of modern sophisticated electronic gadgets, cosmetics, which are thought to be needs rather than luxuries in urban-industrial as well as rural areas have direct repercussion on the Ho economy. These developments are responsible for high expenditure and growing indebtedness, despite a higher level of income. What is, therefore, important is the rise of income among the Ho and not their quality of life.

Changing Political Structure and Leadership

It has been pointed out that the Ho political organization was intimately linked up with the institution of kingship in Mayurbhanj till the Indian independence. But the post-independence introduction of democratic polity with adult franchise and a total restructuring of the political organization have not spared the Ho society, despite their love and attachment to the conventions.

At the village level, the *Pradhan* is no more the political leader, who in almost all cases is replaced by a ward member, the people's representative in the Panchayati system of government. Land tax collection is taken over by the revenue officers, criminal and other law and order situation is looked after by the police and the establishment of social ties, like marriage needs no mediation, as it is decided by the aspirant couple itself. Therefore, for all practical purposes, no administrative or judiciary responsibility is left to the village *Pradhan*. The post, however, perpetuates in most of the Ho villages as an ornamental position, may be for the satisfaction of the visitors to the village. Issues relating to minor offences, like quarrel between the neighbours, debt repayment, encroachment of space, sexual violence etc. are decided by the ward member of the village and in some cases, the Sarpanch is also called for to decide the cases. Although the *Pradhan* remains present in such cases, it is felt that importance is being given to those new political leaders, who pretend themselves as more dynamic.

With the growing politicization of Indian villages, the political wave has not left the tribal villages also. Ideally, the ward member of a Ho village is linked to the total political structure of the country and most often he is well acquainted with the district party workers and the administrative machinery. This has a direct bearing on the development programmes. These political leaders appropriate most of the benefits due to their access to various funding sources and keep on maintaining a separate class of political leaders even in most interior Ho villages.

Changing Religion and Rituals

Like all other aspects of social and cultural life, changes in religious beliefs and rituals among the Ho have been widely observed. These changing traits are very much prominent in urban-industrial areas than in villages due to apparent reasons. Under the influence of modernization the Ho, once a community of the staunch believers of spirits and *bongas*, have started consulting local doctors and visiting nearby government hospitals for common illness. In some cases, relief from the diseases by the modern medical treatment has convinced them to gradually abandon the belief in the malevolent spirits. But the deep seated religious belief has not been completely swayed away, in spite of these gradual changes. Spirit and ancestor worship still continues in many cases till now and they are still believed to be the chief regulators of the Ho life and destiny.

Elaborate and expensive rituals connected with the annual festivals and life-cycle of an individual are no more observed with their usual pomp and splendour. The reason is simple. Most of the annual rituals among the Ho are planned keeping in view the agricultural cycle. The present state of their precarious alienation from the traditional occupation as agriculturists and the preference for wage earning have caused declining significance of these rituals. Important rituals like, *Magh Pudi*, *Ba Parab*, *Hera Parab* etc. are however symbolically observed in many cases. The importance of life-cycle rituals has also greatly declined due to modern forces of change.

Social and ritual superiority of the religious functionaries like *denuri*, *raulla* etc. has been automatically reduced to minimum. A new order in Ho society seems to have emerged, mostly based on rationality and judiciousness.

Agents of Social Change

There are many agents, old and new, which are responsible for bringing about stupendous change in the Ho social structure. The foremost among them is an early industrialization of the district. With huge geological deposits and highly rich in forest resources, the district of Mayurbhanj had drawn the attention of the TISCO and the iron-ore mines of Padampahar, Suleipat and Gorumohisani were the mother-mines for the steel plant at Jamshedpur. Beginning of mining operation had opened new and alluring employment facilities for the communities in close proximity, including that of the Ho. The mining towns, which were cosmopolitan centres with complexity of peoples and cultures, induced the Ho to change their living pattern and social customs. The changes are reflected in their dress pattern, food habits, habitations etc.

Other agents of change are essentially the post-independence developments, encompassing various welfare and developmentally oriented schemes and projects, undertaken by the

Government and a number of voluntary agencies operating in the district. The Community Development blocks in the district achieved the status of Tribal Development blocks due to their large concentration of tribal population and eventually, there was inflow of money for tribal development. Development in education, agriculture, nutrition, health, and family welfare could be taken care of. LAMPS, co-operative societies and commercial banks were opened on a priority basis to promote the objective of tribal development. Villages were taken as the units of benefit, and the Ho automatically came under the purview of the beneficiaries. Out of these, education played a pivotal role in the removal of illiteracy and making them conscious about the developmental benefits. Education has also helped in the rejuvenation of their traditional culture, which was suppressed to some extent by exogenous forces. In the course of interview, one of the Ho informants, an ex-M.L.A., advocated for the consumption of rice-beer, which he compared with their life-source.

One of the powerful agents of change in the life-style of the Ho is the pre-eminence of Hindu impact on the tribe. In the past, when the Ho constituted the militia of the state of Mayurbhanj, they were constantly exposed to the neigbouring Hindu world. This has continued till recently, when the mining employment and industrialization have become a part of their life. Along with their observance of *Magh Pudi* and other conventional festivals, they celebrate Durga Puja, Laxmi Puja etc. like the Hindu castes.

It may finally be said that the Ho society now passes through a transition between tradition and modernity. Although modern forces have changed their life-style to a great extent, their adherence to tradition and maintenance of a Ho cultural identity still continues through these constraints. They have gradually adapted the modern changes, but their satisfaction seems to lie with the old conventions of simple, coordinated living and belief in their sovereign *bongas*.

Appendix I

Kin Terms used among the Ho

Relation	*Term of Address*	*Relation*	*Term of Address*
FF	Tatam	WZ	Tenyaing Kui
MF	Tatam	H el.B	Bau Hanyar
FM	Jian	H yr.B	Eril
MM	Jian	H el.Z	Aji Hanaring
F	Buba	H yr.Z	Eril
M	Maa	WZH	Salagin
FB (el.)	Gungu	H el.BW	Nana
FB (yr.)	Kaka	WBW	Unding/Ajing
F el.BW	Gungu	ZH	Tenyang
F yr.BW	Kaki/Gaen	el.BW	Hili
FZ	Hatom/Jii	yr.ZH	Aratadi
MZ	Kaki/Gaen	yr.BW	Kimin
MZH	Kaka	SWF	Balatadi/Balain
MB	Mamu/Kuman	DHF	Balatadi/Balain
MBW	Hatom/Jii	SWM	Bala era
WF	Hanyar/Mamu	DHM	Bala era
WM	Hanar/Hatom	Son	Han
el.B	Dada/Bau	Daughter	Haning era
yr.B	Undin Kaa	BS	Han
el.Z	Nana	ZS	Han/Gazing
yr.Z	Undin Kui	ZD	Gazing
FBS	Dada/Undin Kaa	SW	Kimin
MZS	Dada/Undin Kaa	SS	Jaain
FZS	Dada/Vndia Kaa	DS	Jaain

FZD	Ajing/Undin Kui	DD	Jaain
FBD	Ajing/Undin Kui	DS	Jaain
MZD	Ajing/Undin Kui	HF	Hanyar
MBS	Dada/Undin Kaa	HM	Hanar/Hatom
MBD	Ajing/Undin Kui		
H	Ham/Hamin		
W	Era		

Appendix II

Names of the Ho *kilis*

Alda
Amang
Andarai

Babanga
Badae
Bage
Banda
Bandia
Bankira
Bansing
Baraj
Baranda
Barda
Bari
Barla
Barmuchu
Bengra
Biruga
Budiuli
Busoi

Chada
Champia
Chark
Chatamba
Chhattar

Dangil
Darai
Dapai
Deogam
Digi

Gadsera
Gaepai
Gagrai
Gilua
Goia

Haiburu
Hanhaga
Hembram
Hesa

Jaj
Jamuda
Jank
Jarika
Jerai

Jori

Kada
Kalundia
Kandakel
Kandeom
Kerai
Kerrah
Kingba
Kudoda
Kuldi
Kulua
Kunkel
Kuntia

Laguri
Lamae
Leangi
Lugum

Melgandi
Merla
Mondoia
Munda
Mundri

Palae
Pingua
Purti

Rakasae

Sae
Sakaesing
Samath
Sambrai
Saonyan
Sasa
Sinku
Sirka
Situ
Sori
Sundi

Taesam
Tikisae
Tiria
Tiu
Tobid
Topno
Toti
Tupusae

Ugursandi

Bibliography

Anderson, W.A. and F.B. Parker	1964	*Social Organization*, New York : D. Van Nostrand Co. Inc.
Bohannan, P. and M. Glazer (ed.)	1973	*High Points in Anthropology*, New York : A.A. Knopf.
Bottomore, T.B.	1962	*Sociology—A Guide to Problems and Literature*, London : George Allen and Unwin Ltd.
Chatterjee, A. and T. Das	1927	*Hos of Seraikella*, Calcutta: Univ. of Calcutta.
Chattopadhyay, G. and S. Biswas	1955	"Annual Festival of Hos", *Man in India*, 35(3), 185-91.
Chattopadhyay, G.	1956a	"Divination of cause of disease among Hos of Seraikella", *Jou. Asiatic Society of Bengal*, 22(S), 5-13.
	1956b	"The festival 'Jatra' or Harmaghe of the Hos", *Jou. Asiatic Soc. of Bengal*, 22(S), 15-19.
	1964	"Kinship and Marriage among the Hos", *Bulletin of the Cultural Res. Inst.*, West Bengal, 3(2), 13.
	1965	"Hos", *Vanyajati*, 13(3), 123-30.

Chattopadhyay, G. and B.C. Roy Choudhari	1957/58	"The Name giving Ceremony of the Hos of Seraikella", *The Eastern Anthropologist*, 11(2), 113-27.
Dalton, E.T.	1872	*Descriptive Ethnology of Bengal*, Calcutta : Govt. Printing Press.
Dasgupta, B.K.	1958	"A Ceremonial Hunting of the Ho in Seraikella", *Adivasi*, 3(2).
Deogan, K.	1928	"A Ho Folkstory", *Man in India*, 8(4), 243-47.
Dhan, R.O.	1961	"The Hos of Saranda", *Bulletin of the Bihar Tribal Res. Inst.*, 3(1).
Evans-Pritchard, E.E.	1979	*Social Anthropology*, London : Routledge and Kegan Paul.
Ginsberg, M.	1947	*Reason and Unreason in Society*, London : W. Heinemann Ltd.
Govt. of India	1955	*The Adivasis*, New Delhi : Ministry of Inf. and Broad.
Griffiths, W.G.	1946	*The Kol Tribe of Central India*, Calcutta : The Royal Asiatic Society of Bengal.
Haldar, S.	1915	"Ho Folklore", *Jou. Bihar and Orissa Res. Society*, 1, 255-73.
Hutton, J.H.	1963	*Caste in India*, Bombay : OUP (4th edn.).
Kuper, A. (ed.)	1977	*The Social Anthropology of Radcliffe-Brown*, London : RKP.
MacIver, R.M. and Page	1962	*Society : An Introductory Analysis*, London : Macmillan & Co. Ltd.

Macpherson, T.S. 1930 "Differences in Customs between the Hos and the Munda in the Singbhum District", *Man in India*, 10, 167-68.

Majumdar, D.N. 1924a "The Traditional Origin of the Hos, together with a brief description of the Chief Bongas (gods) of the Hos", *Jou. and Proc. of the Asiatic Soc. of Bengal*, 20(5), 193-97.

1924b "On the Terminology of Relationships of the Hos of Kolhan", *Jou. and Proc. of the Asiatic Society of Bengal*, 20(5), 199-204.

1925a "Physical Characteristics of the Hos of Kolhan", *Man in India*, 5(3-4), 176-84.

1925b "Some Ethnographic Notes on the Hos of Kolhan", *Man in India*, 5(3-4), 185-92.

1925c "Some Outdoor and Sedentary Games of the Hos of Kolhan", *Man in India*, 5(3-4), 193-202.

1926 "Marriage and Betrothal among the Hos of Kolhan", *Jou. and Proc. of the Asiatic Society of Bengal*, 22(3), 149-68.

1927a "Death and Connected Ceremonies amongst the Hos of Kolhan in Sing-Bhum, *Jou. and Proc. of*

		the Asiatic Society of Bengal, 23, 37-44.
	1927b	"Some of the Worship Festivals of the Hos of Kolhan", *Jou. and Proc. of the Asiatic Society of Bengal*, 23, 277-85.
	1950	*The Affairs of a Tribe*, Lucknow : The Universal Pub. Ltd.
	1954	"Religious Life of the Ho", *Man in India*, 34(4), 346.
Merton, R.K.	1968	*Social Theory and Social Structure*, New Delhi : Amerind Pub. Co. Pvt. Ltd.
Misra, K.K.	1982/83	"Emerging Polity and the Process of Development among the Ho of Orissa", *Manav*, 1(1).
Mitra, S.C.	1917	"Notes on some Ho riddles", *Jou. of the Anthropological Society of Bombay*, 11, 100-119.
Nadel, S.F.	1957	*The Theory of Social Structure*, London : Cohen & West.
Parsons, T. et al (ed.)	1965	*Theories of Society*, New York : The Free Press.
Pradhan, R.K.	1963/64	"Ho", *Adivasi*, 3, 167-70.
Ray, G.S.	1954	"A Magico-religious Ceremony in connection with the disease of a Ho boy", *Man in India*, 34(3), 194-202.
	1960	"Religious Belief of the Hos", *Man in India*, 40(3), 169.

Redfield, R.	1955	*The Little Community*, Chicago : Univ. of Chicago Press.
Risley, H.H.	1891	*Tribes and Castes of Bengal*, Vol. I, Calcutta.
Russel, R.V.	1975	*Tribes and Castes of the Central Provinces of India*, Vol. III, Delhi: Cosmo (First edn. in 1916).
Sahu, R.	1951	"Ho", *Tribes of India*, Part II, New Delhi : B.A.S.S.
Sarkar, G.S.	1916	"Ho Riddles", *Jou. of the Bihar and Orissa Res. Society*, 2, 350-55.
	1918	"Birth and Funeral Ceremonies among the Hos", *Journal of the Bihar and Orissa Res. Society*, 5, 134-42.
Senapati, N. (ed.)	1967	*District Gazetteer, Mayurbhanj*, Cuttack : Govt. Press.
Shukla, N.K.	1976	*The Social Structure of an Indian Village*, Delhi : Cosmo.
Singh, C.P.	1978	*The Ho Tribe of Singbhum*, New Delhi : Classical.
Singh, Y.	1980	*Social Stratification and Change in India*, Delhi : Manohar.

REPORTS

Allen, B.C.	"Ho", *Census of India*, 1901, Vol. 4: Assam, Part I.
O'Malley, L.S.S.	"Ho", *Census of India*, 1911, Vol. 5 : Bengal, Bihar, Orissa and Sikkim, Part I.

Tallents, P.C.	"Ho", *Census of India*, 1921, Vol. 3 : Bihar and Orissa, Part I.
Porter, A.E.	"Ho", *Census of India*, 1931, Vol. 5 : Bengal and Sikkim, Part I.
M. Laeequddin	"Kol (Ho)", *Census of Mayurbhanj State*, 1931, Vol. I.
Mitra, A.	"Ho", *Census of India*, 1951, West Bengal.

Index